ISBN: 9798480830880 (Paperback)

Printed by amazon.us, in the United States of America.

First Printing,2021.

E&E-Publishings,LLC
PO Box 652
Blue Island, Illinois 60406
www.vanceestes1@icloud.com

CONTENTS

- Lost Souls-Buried Alive
- Money Pit-Incarceration Costs
- Return On Investment-Tax Dollars
- Generation Genocide-Last Of A Dying Breed
- Born Losers-A Future Unfulfilled
- Birth Of a Monster-Society's Creation
- Civil Death-Return To Society
- Ball and Chains-My Own Oppressions
- Whip Wounds & Scars-PTSD & Emotional Turmoil
- The Hurt Keeps Hurting-Cycle of Victimization
- Conscious For The Unconscious-Understanding The Destructive Impact
- War Machine-Recognizing The Battlefield
- Braising Cattle-Fictitious Freedom
- World War $-Poor vs Rich
- Fom Bondage To Billions-Combining Black Wealth
- Regrets.Reflect.Reapply.-Starting Over
- Sweet Nightmares-Wake Up or Sleep Forever
- Breaking Branches-What Needs To Happen

Preface

For decades utterly silenced by society, and discounted by my peers; I feel its my mission duty that I speak for millions of souls in this book done the same way, a voice beyond the cell walls and emotional imprisonment that they are unsure of how to break free from. Also I write to give a voice to my motives and reasons for sins of man and crimes against society; to vindicate my character from misrepresentation. As a prisoner myself, I feel obliged to give you an observation of the sufferings thats continued to be the narrative of so many black and brown people. Them being my primary motive in writing this book; to help the outside world understand the depth of our struggles to redemption.

Undoubtedly, the pathway to glory is rough. I sincerely hope that you may never have to experience the humility that the power of the American Government has reduced me to. There is no intent to give a history lesson, but a modern day perspective of the justice system horrors and aggressive racism from an account of one who's suffered in it, and through it. This book is not intended to identify all of the racial issues of the region nor to explore the depths of each of those issues. There's more than enough to write an entire book on a single symptom. Today is the results from yesterday.

Because I'm from a drug game culture period, decidedly I'ma sell you a kilo gram worth of solid perspective literature information plus tax. These chapters are broken down to 36 ounce chapters, each chapter ounce will contain 28 gram pivotal point perspectives in each gram, give or take, it is so you can understand the purity of the game being sold to you on a daily basis. Whether you believe you're part of the game being played on you is entirely your opinion. If you know this game, then you're probably a p ayer, or if you're like me, then you're the loser in it. Meant to lose and designed to lose in it. You may ask yourself; "Well How Can I Win?", but first I want you to ask yourself; how can you beat a game you don't realize you're playing in?

1

The White Plague—Destination:Death & Destruction

Among early sixteenth century inhabitants, In various countries of Europe and American colonies, there were white people too proud and lazy to work their own lands and fields procured, but yet desirous to dress in the best and live on the fat of the land. At the direction of brutal Spanish sailors involved in the business of slave trading human souls as a means of commerce. They sent ships to Africa to bring them natives, whom they compelled to work without wages, limited scant food, and scarcely any clothing. Italian sailor, Christopher Columbus, voyages opened up the Americas to centuries of exploitation, death and misery for millions of native peoples at the hands of Europeans. The cruel policy of enslavement and killing initiated by Columbus and pursued by his successors resulted in complete genocide. These whites grew rich on the labor of these natives, and spent their own time in drinking, gambling, and raping the women slaves.

Slave traders, in order to supply them with as many African natives as they wanted, would kidnap all the men, women, and children they could catch on the coast of west Africa; and would buy others from the chiefs of African villages that were taken as prisoners of war conflicts, paying them mostly in rum and gun powder. This practice made the different tribes desirous to go to war with each other, in order to take more prisoners to sell to the white slave traders.

This mean and cruel business has been carried on by white men for four hundred years; and all that while African villages of men, women, and children were carried off to hopeless slavery in distant lands. Continual violence, and intercourse with such ruthless white men as the slave traders, kept the Africans barbarous; and made them much more barbarous than they would otherwise have been. Such a state of things made it impossible for them to improve their civilization standards, as they would have done if the white nations calling themselves Christians had sent them literature books and bibles instead of rum; teachers instead of slave traders; and tools and machinery instead of gun powder.

The heinous stealing of men, women, and children from their homes, torturing them on the ocean trike to America, and selling them in strange lands, to whipped to incessant toil without wages continued on in this fashion has a normalcy act of business commerce for centuries. But African natives were not the only race subjected to the white race spreading seizure.

Long before Europeans came to the area and before they brought back captives, there were already inhabitants living here. Just like before Christopher Columbus stumbled upon South America, native tribes had been in the region for thousands of years. Native Americans were the first victims of land theft and people removal. These first slaves of white men,Native Indians.

Slavery existing from the time of the early exploration and settlement of the region by the French. Though it is true that the Red Men usually chose death rather than slavery. It could not contend with the want for more country land that they had now become found of, and decimating the Native American tribes through slavery, war, and diseases would prove to be the genocidal methods useful to use. Pitting already waring native tribes against one another. Hired native Indians to fight against Indians, and sat back while many natives were destroyed.

When the guns, strong liquors, diseases brung in hadn't slain enough thousands, they forced their religion upon natives in effort to maintain control and dominate with missionaries. The native Red Man only offense was that they owned land in which whites wanted. These whites were a wretched and degenerate race, cowardly, treacherous, filthy and indolent. Slaves of native Indian and African nations were very hardy and could perform with ease labors which many white men would shrink from.

The enslavement of the Blackman by the whites from the early part of the eighteenth century became more and more extensive along the Mississippi and lower Louisiana settlement territories. The abolishment of slavery shortly after the civil war seem to do little to the violence black people were subjected to. The ordinance of 1784 was antecedent to the more important ordinance of 1787, which carried the famous sixth article the neither slavery nor involuntary servitude except as a punishment for crime should exist in the Northwest Territory. Both Illinois and Indiana States finally but gradually incorporated into their constitutions compromise provisions for a nominal prohibition of slavery in keeping with the spirit of the majority who framed the const tution, despite the fact that the indenture system in southern Illinois and especially in Indiana was at times tantamount to slavery as it was practiced in parts of the south.

Black people were more detested in the free states than in those where they were held as slaves. By the time the second great migration after the first phase from 1910-1930 that attracted rural blacks to leave the south in droves. Up north, racial tensions increased over jobs and housing. Many moved to St.Louis, Chicago, Detroit, Philly and even further north to New York. Streams of hopeful African descendants with little personal resources came looking for the "Promised Land" in St.Louis and instead were crowded into segregated spaces with poor city services such as sanitation. They lacked access to health facilities and employment. These ghettos, created by racist policies, became the justification for future real estate steering, zoning restrictions and redlining.

The 1917 East St.Louis race riot was a grim reminder for the new arrivals to keep on pushing northward or westward. An estimated 150-200 blacks were killed in east boogie and 6000 blacks were left homeless when their neighborhoods were burned to the ground by white mobs. It's a tired, old narrative the never loses its potency when it comes to white people don't want black neighbors. Destroying their accumulated property and beating them mercilessly. White policemen, who initial duties were designed to protect matters of property, gave rise to the most accessories to violent contacts with blacks.

This rise in relations foretells that everywhere the White man sets his sights, over consumption from domination follows until the environment suffers, rather its the species or surrounding nature. The white race nations to this day has still not made apologies for these atrocities committed, but implies it can be trusted against the very signs of its nature. Being so much similar to the story of the scorpion and the turtle at the river bed about to cross when the scorpion ask the turtle, who had no problem in crossing, could he get on his back in order to make it safely across the river from drowning. At first request the turtle denied him; pointing out his nature to sting in the back of the neck while the victim wasn't paying attention trustingly, but granted the request after the scorpion promised he wouldn't. Just before making it to the other side of the river bed, the scorpion struck the turtle in the back of the neck as he jumped off and the turtle now drowning to his peril said; "But you promised me you wouldn't sting me"! To this the scorpion replied; "And you actually believed and trusted me, it's in my nature".

2

Hanging Tree Seeds-The Setup

One most understanc the dynamics to be consciously aware of the expected end results. Africa is four thousand miles across the Atlantic Ocean from the United States. It is inhabited by numerous tribes of black people, each tribe with a separate government. These tribes vary in degrees of intelligence and civilization. Formerly the African Chiefs sold men into slavery only in punishment for some crime they had committed, or to work out a debt they hac failed to pay, or because they were prisoners taken in war. These customs were barbarous enough, but they were not so bad as what they were afterward taught to do by nations calling themselves Christians. A religion grossly intended to drop the guards of intended targets and become docile and obedient.

In 1830 blacks were excluded from service in the state militia, in 1831 they were deprived of the privilege of serving on juries, and in 1838 they were denied the right of having their children educated at the expense of the state. Whenever possible the free states enacted laws to prevent or discourage the influx of free blacks and to restrict the privileges of those already there. I point to Illinois as willing to accept this unusual influx of members of another race passed the drastic law of 1853 prohibiting the immigration. It provided for the prosecution of any person bringing a negro into the state and also for arresting and fining any negro $50, should he appear there and remain longer than ten days. If he proved to be unable to pay the fine, he could be sold to any person who could pay the cost of the trial.

Additionally, white mobs regularly attacked homes of blacks and forced out of settlement communities during the 1800's. Blacks themselves had no land, no mules, no farming or industrial equipment, and they could not acquire sufficient capital to obtain these things. Whites continued further to make blacks sufferings in consequent privations and want aggravated by robbery, rapes, and murder by the Ku Klux Klan. Persevering still, after the Civil War, the few blacks where investments in real estate opportunities were possible, lost their political power, also had their property seized on the pleas for delinquent taxes and they were forced into the ghetto of towns and cities, as it became a crime punishable by social proscription to sell blacks desirable residences. The aim to debase all blacks to the status of menial labor in conformity with the usual contention of the south that slavery is the normal condition of the blacks.

Along with these oppressions came the institution of the credit system, which furnished the capstone of the economic structure so harmful to blacks and other poor people. This system makes poor blacks dependent for their living on an advance of supplies of food, clothing or tools during the year, secured by a lien on the property owned or paycheck wages earned. The consistent stream of oppressions give blacks no chance to learn business methods during the days of slavery, and even now still they fall a prey to loan sharks, and established stores everywhere in impoverished communities to exhort their income means before it can be gathered and ownership of property by the mischievous credit system that charged two to three times as much in interest and contract fees. This evil system still reigns supreme in communities of color and induces the lost of ambition to become land or home owners, preferring to invest their surplus money in personal effects; and the few who are induced to undertake the buying of land, they often tire of the responsibility and give it up.

New evils became ever more evident after the progressive steps instituted to end slavery, and implement black persons rights here in America with the 1964 Civil Rights Bill. A new method of slave oppression had to be created to not only halt progress, but also discourage further ambitions.

3

Slave Schools–
Miseducation Protocol

The suppression of economic knowledge is a corrupt motive being as clear as the motive of a drug dealer for concealing his drugs from a policeman. In society, the lower the type, and the less cultivated the mind, the less courage there is to face important subjects objectively. Making the average man possess no real individuality. Instituted systemic work of intimidating blacks into submission to the domination of the whites. A plan at the same time directing the development of blacks in such a way that they would never become the competitors of the white people. Unable to obtain liberal education at the level of public school systems, consequently, added to blacks misfortunes, although they themselves as the largest consumers in some parts, pay most of the taxes appropriated to the support of schools for the youth of the other race.

Inner city American Public School systems aimed at miseducating its youth to the atrocities its committed in the past that has ultimately been its benefactor in instituting its current modern civilization. School books and lesson plans purposely designed to white wash history accounts and disproportionately provide inadequate funcing to urban area schools for qualified teachers and books and relevant life skill lessons in Law, Money, and Love. Law as its relevance to everyday life; Money as it pertains to investing, property, and entrepreneurial earnings; Love in building a family, emotional health and relationships.

Mental nourishment is quite as necessary as physical nourishment. Slavery itself was to be blamed for discouraging education of blacks. Whites did practically nothing to remove the underlying causes that impeded proper schooling systems to be created for blacks after slavery abolished. The earliest history of schools for blacks were affiliated with churches and states began making educating blacks-slave or free-illegal in 1847. The fight for quality education would consume African Americans for generations. Most states general assembly doesn't seem to have the political will or the capacity to get to the root of failing schools. The lack of proactive policies are pushing our youth into low-wage jobs or into the Prison Industrial Complex.

After the historic case of Brown vs. The Broad of Education, the public school system in much regards took on an unspoken regard as much horrible than prison. It is in some respects more cruel than a prison. But in a prison for instance, you are not forced to read books written by the wardens and governors and beater or otherwise tormented if you cannot remember their utterly unmemorable content product of an organized education plan.

In prison you are not forced to sit listening to turn-keys discoursing without charm or interest on subjects that they don't understand and don't care about, and are therefore incapable of making you understand or care about the learning material placed in front of you.

In a prison they may torture your body; but they do not torture your brains. In a school you are forced to read a hideous imposture of learning material and historic accounts, all the while the worlds bookshelves are loaded with truth, fascinating and inspiring books. This is not education but fabrication. It is destruction, not development. Real education would consist in assisting every individual to train to their highest capacity for any special talents that might reveal themselves during the process.

Above all things, real education would encourage the utilization of the brain for purposes of thought and reflection, instead of trying to make it a warehouse for storing pallet-loads of useless knowledge. The aim should be to rouse, strengthen, and illumine the mind rather than to store it with learning; and the great educational system problem has been void of catering to develop it.

If progress means ideas, then mediocrity does not deal in them. Our educational systems are busily engaged in the work destroying individual genius development, substituting facts for opinionated ideas, forcing the mind away from its natural course, and manufacturing a machine fit for a lifetime of employment instead of a man self-made to create new industries, new ideas, and change.

A man knows best what he has taught himself. The greatest statesman, philosophers, scientists, writers, and other men of genius have been self-made or self-cultured. But whites wont recognize your skill sets and abilities if not indoctrinated under their educational systems. Through this enforced attempt ,it will make you loathe the sight of a book all the rest of your life.

Personally, none of my school teachers carried with them the enthusiastic attitude to teach knowledgable lessons. This not a care attitude of whether I learnt my lessons or not, consequently swayed my attentions to other personal home matters and the streets. I ask; how can a student properly receive an education if he's hungry because theirs no food at home? If he's distracted by the insecurities of his tattered apparel because his family can't afford decent clothes to dress him in, how can he focus on receiving that education properly? He is at school during the day but when he'll return home he'll be subjected to a war-zone in the evening. All the more tragic but common circumstances for black youth.

Children need room to think; their minds have to grow up as well as their bodies. Without a free and open mind there is no high and glad human life. Only the man who is really contended and happy can have his mind free to receive teaching well. I would have to teach myself through various life experiences over the years of adulthood what should have originally taught to me in my developing youth.

4

Trojan Horses–False Idols

When Moses went atop of Mount Sinai to speak with God he returned to find his followers had quickly in disarray constructed a golden altar to worship and in all intentions to follow in his absence. Moses then destroyed the false idol and rebuked the followers for worshiping a false god after have already given them clear signs as to the rightful and only god they shall worship and hold most high. On this long journey, a many of gods children have lost their way and fell victim to figures instilled in the camps of the oppressed at the direction of the oppressors. They come in many forms: as a leader; social idol; and even as a liberator, but yet and still, their job will be to lead you to your slaughter.

In the places of the leaders who wont speak for their people, the whites have raised up blacks who accept favors offered to them on the condition that they direct the main issues as to the rights of blacks away from the forefront. This in turn, makes you feel comfortable as a whining baby being rocked back to sleep, quickly to forget your ever surmounting problems thats not being cured and rarely treated.

These false leaders, who preach with no actions or results to show, are all smoke and mirrors. They come in many forms of preachers who minister to gather your trust , and hard earned money, but live a life of luxury totally abandoned from what they preach mean while you, a mesmerized follower live poor, anxiously and persistently praying for a better day. These preachers, armed with the gift of gab rather than any gifts from god, take full advantage of the poor peoples vulnerability and ignorance. Getting his audience and pay on the condition that he stoop to the gossip which centers around new theories, startling events, and ongoings in the country. His sole agenda is to receive money by those willing to be entertained and amused, led astray on hopes, as he profits off their pain and poverty.

In times of great social and economic crises these leaders will have an insurmountable amount of the people afflicted the greatest marching the streets and discussing the issues instead of revolting against the proprietors they've made rich off their sufferings or lobbying bills into law that would protect them from further injury, rather its physical or financial. They'll rally the battle cries of a few but effect the majority the greatest negatively.

Issues of slavery descendants reparations fall on deaf ears over the past century in light of segregated housing and schools. False idols will step up begging the same oppressors for aid and assistance resulting in dependency instead of self-efficiency; integration instead of separation.

Matters of racial profiling, police brutality, and cop shootings of unarmed black men will be overlapped in news and media outlets with the crimes of a few blacks. Programmed citizens aiding the cycles of destruction with lobbied laws to increase sentences for crimes until someone they love is negatively affected by it.

Just recently over the past decade, gun crimes were used as a propaganda platform to initiate more severe racially bias laws against persons caught in possession of a gun. So much severe the the original persons who initially favored these laws retracted their opinions and support when it was their own family members and community neighbors who began to be negatively affected by them in mass incarceration amounts.

Upheld community leaders rally for the removal of drugs and gang violence from the black communities but public school funding and more job opportunities go unchecked. Instances of the crack epidemic was responded with the 1982 Crime Bill targeting mainly black and poor community residents. These voted for democrats who were mainly supported by blacks to win office positions, once elected produced lobbied bills that made coke to crack ratio of small amounts of just 5 grams of crack possession or more, a minimum 5 year prison sentence term.

These same detrimental leaders also pursued drafted bills that reinstitute the death penalty for drug trafficking offenses at the Federal level, and Civil Forfeiture seizure of all valuable property owned that can now be taken away under these laws.

The very reasons of black drug dealers was the opportunities to take advantage of rising out of their oppressive circumstances they've been subjected to, never has there been malice attempts in intentions but ignorance of the totality of drug addictions devastating affects it would have on the people around them.

A decade later these same leaders lobbied an additional blow to black communities with the 1994 Crime Bill that provided billions in funding to states to employ and increase more police on the streets to aggressively go after communities of color; to build more prisons; and to incentivize states to create harsher sentences for drug crimes. But no bills lobbied equally for the creation of jobs to combat the rising unemployment. No bills from these false leaders to build new schools, hire more better trained teachers, or improve learning materials and after-school programs and build expansive housing to combat the overcrowded project ghettos cramped with poor people prone to commit crime in order to eat, have shelter, and survive.

This targeted Criminal Justice overhaul had devastating effects on black communities, resulting in the U.S. having the largest prison population than any where else in the world, w th more than 2 million people incarcerated, and another 2 million on some form of probation, parole, or supervised release creating a mass incarceration epidemic. The racial sentencing disparities cannot be ignored with 80% of inmates across the U.S. prisons being African Americans. Most fail to realize that it's been the democratic party seeking to keep the poor poor and blacks without Civil Rights and disagreed originally with the abolishment of slavery.

Better leaders are the heads of households well into diminishing yearly because of confinement. Fathers of families of whole communities vanishing, leaving the women and children to fend for themselves. If there is to be change, it must come from within. Each person a leader leading himself to positive progress along with his family, community and village and so forth independently; and recognizing the unfulfilled promises of better described illusionists rather than leaders.

5

Martyred Heroes– Assassinated Greats

Dr. Martin Luther King had a dream. I have a vision, a plan with a goal in mind and progressive efforts to get there strong and steadily. One can take pride in Dr. King, Malcolm X, and Toussaint L'Overture, as some of the men who made an opening of freedom for their oppressed race, and by the greatness of his character and achievements proved the capabilities of black men. A willing sacrifice for the multitude if not by just minimally encouragement and bravery in spirit.

Gallantly Toussaint L'Overture went to his demise after liberating St. Domingo,Haiti of slavery on the island. The spark of revolution also struck fear in the French who reacted horribly violent to the new sought independence, and per Commander Napoleon Bonaparte orders, every where colored men were seized and executed without forms of law. General Toussaint L'Overture most distinguished General Maurepas, after Toussaint's kidnapping, was strung up by spikes in his shoulders to a ship vessel, to watch as his wife and children, and four hundred of his black soldiers, were thrown over to the sharks before his eyes. Inland trees were hung with the corpses of blacks. Some were torn to pieces by bloodhounds trained for the purpose; some were burnt alive. Sixteen of Toussaint's bravest Generals were chained by the neck to the rocks of an uninhabited island, and left there to perish.

Most of these victims were firm in the midst of their tortures, and died with the precious word "Freedom" on their lips. A unrelenting earnest desire to escape slavery and its barbarities undoubtedly burned within Harriet Tubman to make the multiple dangerous trikes north. In her bravery, she also showed other slaves the way to escape towards freedom. As a natural born light beacon of hope for others to follow and be inspired to live up to. The same beacon of hope shone from Fredrick Douglas publications; from Dr. King speeches; and Nelson Mandela, and Malcolm X redemptions from the chains of confinement.

I relate more with the challenges and triumphs of Malcolm X more than any other historic figure I've come to learn of. His bravery resonates with my spirit on the journey of redemption through temptations and misunderstandings. To see soon the error of my ways, and resolved to reform. I refuse to be categorized for the mistakes of my past, and let my story end there without correction. The forethought of people remember you more for your actions rather than your intentions.

In 1831, Nate Turner, a black slave in Virginia, led a local slave rebellion, starting August 21st. 57 whites were killed, and troops were called in, and 100 slaves were killed. Turner was captured, tried and hanged November 11th. The bravery of Nate Turner will forever inspire courage in the hearts of black people, and a stain of fear in the hearts of whites. To him, it was plain that his people must resist their tyrants, or be forever hopelessly crushed. By becoming a leader he felt that he might protect the ignorant masses, and restrain those who were disposed to cruelty. A thought that he was the appointed deliverer, a second Moses, sent by God to bring his people out of bondage. From that time henceforth he made it the business of his life to conquer freedom for his race; but even in a blood thirsty spirit, driven to desperation, became as cruel as their oppressors, with all the barbarities they had seen and suffered.

Though naturally of a mild disposition. These circumstances will make for being perfectly crazy with revenge, thenceforth having no mercy on anyone of white complexion. Even John Brown as a devoted man who believed in the liberty of slaves, took up his gun in hand and raised it in rebellion against the country. Though tried, convicted and hanged for murder under the laws of man, but under the laws of God he was a hero.

To be loyal to a cause is the finest tribute that can be paid to any man. When a stipid Government system, grasping our reverence for fidelity, tried to ban our heroes by calling them felons, thugs, and murders; loyalty is the fine attribute of the fine nature. We fight for freedom, not for the hope of material profit or comfort, but because every fine instinct of manhood demands that man be free and life beautiful and brave. A man who revolts to win his freedom is the same as he who dies to defend it. He is loyal always and most wonderfully lovable, because in the darkest times, when banned as wild, wicked, and rebel, he is loyal still as from the beginning, and will be to the end.

6

Divide & Conquer-
Brother Against Brother

It's the oldest form of war tactic to make use of. In this opportunity, you can infiltrate and destroy the opposition to oblivion without a single shot fired. Why do the work that someone else can do for you? Instead the modern day sinister white man has recognized a profound discovery in which he can attribute to the same discovery four centuries earlier in Africa and in America. The enemy of my enemy is my friend.

Upon gracing West Africa, native tribes were in centuries old conflicts with one another, always too busy fighting among themselves. The same can be held true about Native American Tribes. These conflicts provided an opportunity for white slavers to capitalize on the distraction and allow for further separation, death, and destruction by providing advance weapons to both fighting sides but more in abundance to the side in which he had greater interest in to win for his benefit. The most likely reason being lives for the slave trade and land for settlement then.

African Natives captured rival waring tribesman as prisoners of war, and at the white slavers request, traded those captives to them for small goods. Indian-Americans followed the same custom, ignorant of the dire and sinister motive it was intended for. Fast forward to present date, violence within Urban communities are no different than tribal conflicts within nations of native people pre-dating European and Spanish settlers influences here in the U.S. and Africa. Peoples behavior today is a Bi-product of their history, as history usually reveals itself again in one form or another.

Today's Poor men, warrior in character in its best aspect, brave, patriotic, and eloquent, faithful and loyal as friends, but terrible as enemies. Men who have a great passion for war. Wars undertaken for revenge rather than conquest. To forgive an injury is considered a shame. Revenge being the noblest of virtues. Also in today's youths are aggression and frustration. It is misguided, directed inward at self and those closest to him. Throw in the mass distribution mix of Guns, Drugs, and Alcohol into poverty and you amplify the violence, crime, and destruction.

It's easily noticeable that theres abundant liquor stores in communities of color. Drugs produced in foreign countries are easily found in Urban cities across the U.S. Truck loads of machine guns and automatic weapons are shipped threw poor communities and make their way into the hands of its residents.

Poor people labeled violent offenders now with this cocktail, and still no one refers to the crimes of mass murders and serial killers like Jeffrey Dahmer and Ted Bundy as being "White-on-White" crimes. Only people of African descent have been made to believe that something is inherently different about the way we commit crimes against one another by suggesting it as being "Black-on-Black' crimes.

To pit brother against his brother is an inapt thing that goes against human nature. But on closer reflection it would align right along with human nature. Kane and Able taken as a prime example. The stage as already been set up for war but to recognize that you are only being played as pawns in the grand scheme of things will take greater effort. We have too often fallen to furiously fighting with one another instead of concerning ourselves more with the common enemy. In battle, soldiers walk over the dead bodies of friends and foes alike unmoved, the only thought being the desire to win, not questioning the point of the war in of itself. A trust mislead. A brainwashed belief to think you should eliminate a person in the same struggle as you.

Mirrored distrust in people who don't trust people but always end up trusting the wrong people. You'll pick up a gun against your own kind but throw it down and give up your rights when the oppressor comes around; bow down and suck up to him for favor crumbs, but treat your own kind like shit. It's a cowards move.

The constant barrage of drugs and alcohol dissolve the thought process to find the resolve through all the weariness compounded on the body and brain by struggle, worry, and strife—all products of poverty and oppression applied. Few find themselves victorious in the battle of life, even fewer stop to inquire of themselves the means they are taking to attain their way. Many who, in their desire to win at all hazards to their integrity and dignity, walk over the bodies of fallen friends, now created enemies, in all weary hearted efforts to succeed in reaching the top most rung of the white man's ladder, instead of building his own. Some have taken a step higher by walking over the body of a brother who has fallen by the wayside, ignoring the groans of the struggling drowned in the exultant shouts of the successful to glorify its own demise.

Hip-Hop/Gangster rappers unfortunately intensifies these false perceptions to a lifestyle they haven't or don't live but others idolize and want to portray and does actually to replicate; shoot guns, sell drugs, murder and rob people, abuse drugs, and demoralize our women; and pit brother against brother.

A step further is taken with man against woman and vice versa. Man in all intentions tries immensely to provide for his family in oppressive circumstances. In some cases of the black mans struggles, the compounding stress of the given responsibilities and challenges against him will destroy his resolve into a slow death, putting him into fight or flight mode to deal with them. His anger will be projected back onto his woman and children, or he'll flee away from his circumstances because the stress, and frustration, will become too intense to manage a presence around.

We have a whole generation of fathers that said; "Fuck It", I'm not gone raise my kids because of this. The role of a black woman should not be sole head of the household. She is that way because we have given her no other choice. It takes a man to accept responsibility and too many are too lazy, and too caught up in other things to do that. As a result, we lose our families, we create young men who lack direction and young women with no structure, and the end result is a cycle of nothingness.

Women especially, have sometimes a most object-able habit of hurling home truths at their husbands head covered in insults whenever tempers run high; and most men are sensitive enough under their shield of cultivated indifference to resent this behavior acutely, and remember every stinging comment of this kind for years. The fact that they are generally true does not make them less offensive. Some wives who are in reality devoted to their husbands, nevertheless make a point of invariably belittling them in private and public, and, though he would rarely admit it, this takes the heart out of a man more than one unknowledgeaole in hearts of men could possibly believe. The truth is men like admiration and praise just as much as women do, though it is part of their makeup to conceal this. They resent a snub just as bitterly as a woman does.

The women was in most tribes the head of the house. She exerted great influence in public matters of the tribe. A husband confides in her for decisions leading the question peace and war. To her the children belong. If she were dissatisfied with her husband, she would drive him from the house and bid him return to his mother. If a man were lazy or failed to bring in plenty of game and fish, he was quite sure to be cast off. But the black woman's equal anger , frustration, and bitterness, keeps the foot on the black mans neck just as much as their oppressor. And in the immortal words of Vin Diesel: "The problem with putting your foot on a Tiger's neck is thats where you'll have to keep it".

Respect and courtesy goes a long way. In this vast universe there is room for all, no need to slander your brother of the same struggle with envious tongues. If he succeeds while you fail, it will not better your condition to slander and vilify; if he fails while you win you will never regret having offered the hand in goodwill and fellowship. Respect holds nation together above love, compatibility, loyalty, and through the most trying disagreements. You must cultivate respect at all costs. Courtesy follows respect and a great deal of bitterness would be saved if this were studiously remembered instead of carrying sneers and taunts to jostle your fellow man and neighbor. Claims of courtesy would prevent all sorts of remarks that belong to the category of the better-left-unsaid. It is when they find out that it is better to be peaceful and work to help each other, then they will be able to grow wise and strong like the other nations. Recognize the common enemy and join forces as a combined regiment instead of a divided nation. Let us be loyal in the deep sense, and let us not be afraid of being few at first. An earnest band is more effective than a discreditable multitude.

7

Who Am I?–
Culture Identity Deletion

Superior power seems only to produce superior brutality. Even when blacks accepted the notion of segregated housing and hence, segregated neighborhoods, they still found themselves under attack or at the whim of urban renewal or "Negro Removal". Whether it was segregated housing developments or segregated neighborhoods or segregated towns, the goal seemed to be the same: to dismantle, to disrupt, dislocate the history, culture and institutions of African Americans.

In recognizing the consistent efforts since slavery to remove ancient languages, the whitewashing of written and spoken history, ancestry lineages, and any knowledge of self pegs a define question as to why. Why are you so threaten by me learning my true existence, my true greatness, and true supremacy?

White writers, historians, and scholars would lead youth to believe that slavery, with its forced transportation to America, was a necessary step in the training of the "Negro" into a more favorable position for development than he has ever before been offered. It's this racist ignorance that whites use in justifying its barbaric shameful actions. The importation of slaves into America ought to be a subject of the deepest regret; to every benevolent and thinking mind. A repugnant to the feelings of nature, and inconsistent with the original rights of man.

Going through the majority of American History books produced by white authors and white owned publishing companies, would leave one with the impression that the black race has not created anything of historic significance and never has. The African and Native American tribesman were just a rudimentary and primitive civilization of savages, instead of respecting another race culture development stage, and not to treat them as inferior, but acknowledging their choice to live as the way they please. What gives anyone the right to decide whether another race customs were wrong because it was different from their own?

Much confusion is related to a many people who aren't necessarily of African descendant, but of native tribes, coupled together as part of the same struggles and oppressions. Many black slaves found refuge among native reservations when escaping slavery cruelty's. I myself, a descendant of the aboriginal Native American people, French, and of African heritage.

Through my own relentless studying, research, and tedious inquiries did I discover this. A lot more of black society aren't given the opportunity to peaceably reflect, research, and refer their generational knowledge to their children because of constant streams of struggles dividing their attention to these much needed details. Now you have a generation lost and embittered immensely projected inwardly among society. Given this standard of living one can understand the source of our legitimate outrage—the unbated humiliation, assaults and murders of black humanity with little or no accountability or impunity.

It is a multitude of the black population who doesn't know their ancestral history past their great grandmothers, even less their fathers side because of death, imprisonment, or drugs; difficulty in tracing roots because African natives were stripped of their names and forced to hold the title names of slave owners. Even today, blacks are stigmatized and prejudiced against by employers, and other blacks, because of having what's considered black names before they're given the opportunity of fair introduction. As a result continue to take on the names given by slave masters in an effort not to be frowned or prejudged upon.

There are as many nationalities of Africans as is various nations of Native Americans. Africa in its vastness was exploited by the white nations growing in civilization for the enormous wealth of gold, ivory, coal, diamonds, platinum, oil, cocoa, slaves, and other raw materials. Had the many nations of Africa combined as one united country and recognized its own natural land wealth, it would be the wealthiest and most powerful country in the entire world. It is quite possibly that is why that the white man has always rule Africa with a strong hand. It wil be a bad day for the white man when the black man rules.

America, prior to European settlers, in of its vast virgin forests, contained some of the same land wealth in raw materials of gold, oil, coal, cotton, and native men, ignorant of their real intentions. As a timeline it has been in their very nature to rob, kill, and destroy.

The U.S. has a long history of sinister deception and theft:

•In 1626, Manhattan Island was "purchased" from Native Americans for goods valued at $24.

•The 1676 brutal Indian War in New England in which King Phillip, Wampanoag Chief, and Narragansett Indians were killed, and 23 planter followers of Nathaniel Brown against British Governor Sir.William Berkeley.

•A 1683 Treaty forced Delaware Indians to accept a pence for Pennsylvania lands

•In 1704, Indians and French allies attacked Deerfield, MA. On February 29, killing 40, capturing and marched off 100.

•The 1795 Treaty of Greenville with Indians and General Wayne opened Northwest Territory to settlers, but same year U.S. brought peace from Algerian pirates by paying a $1Million dollar ransom for 115 seaman September 5th followed by annual tributes.

•In 1814, troops under Andrew Jackson orders defeated Creek Indians led by Chief Wheatherford at Battle of Horseshoe Bend in Alabama, March 29, ending the Creek Indian War which began a year earlier.

•Now, President Jackson, in 1830, signed the Indian Removal Act, granting the President authority to negotiate treaties whereby Indians living east of Mississippi River would give up their lands in exchange for accepting lands in the west.

•The Blackhawk War of 1832 in Illinois and Wisconsin, April through September pushed Sauk and Fox Indians west across the Mississippi.

•Seminole Indians in Florida under Osceola, began attacks November 1,1835, protesting the forced removal. It was the same year gold was discovered on Cherokee land in Georgia. Indians were forced to cede lands December 20th, and to cross the Mississippi.

•In 1838, Cherokee Indians were forced to walk in what is known as the "Trail Of Tears", from southeast U.S. to an area in present-day Oklahoma. At least 4,000, nearly one-fifth of the Cherokee population, are estimated to have perished.

•General William Tecumseh Sherman, in 1864, marched through Georgia taking Atlanta on September 1st, and Savannah December 22th.

•In the Sand Creek Massacre of Cheyenne and Arapaho Indians, November 29th, soldiers drove Indians out the village, killing 150.

•The 1876 Battle of the Little Big Horn,MT, in the Sioux Indian War. Col.George A Custer and 264 soldiers of the 7th cavalry were killed June 25 in a last stand offense.

•Apache Indian Geronimo surrendered September 4th, 1886, ending the last major Indian war.

•In 1889, the U.S. opened 2 million acres of the Oklahoma district to settlers April 22nd, initiating land runs; but "sooner" settlers illegally entered the territory before that date to stake favorable claims-pushing Indians further out westward.

One must objectively began to ask; if my culture wasn't so great then why go to so great of lengths to destroy my people through rape, robbery, and murder? Why when friendly offers of trade were intended, yours were laced with deception, and evil and sinister motives? If the Black race never amassed to any great humankind significance, then why conceal my culture historic accounts, rewrite history, and demand initially that it be a crime that Blacks should read, write, and speak their native tongue?

So great of the White race, it keeps all other none white nations oppressed so systematically and controlled. To not know oneself is to not know your capabilities, strengths, and advantages. To constantly instill into someone that they'll never amount to anything just because the color of their skin leaves them with the lack of motivation to prove otherwise: why try if I'm destined not to amount to anything great?

To steal knowledge from tribal medicine men equally means you lack the knowledge, wisdom, and understanding to attain it yourself. If you adopt the hunting and farming skills of natives in order to survive, equally demonstrates your ignorance of the basic necessities given to human beings. To cruelly subject a person to slave labor shows your deficient in the strength, agility, and ability to complete the very tasks that's savagely applied to another.

In these enlightenments, self-knowledge produces beautiful effects upon the character. Recognizing the adversity subjected to has also increased the resilience within to become wise and great, and begin to try to make things beautiful as well as useful in daily efforts for the greater whole. It is only when a race reaches its maximum of physical development that it arrives at its highest point of energy and moral vigor. But where the identity and ideals of the oppressed is forgotten, they will take on the identity and ideals of the oppressor.

Acknowledge the 40 million souls lost in the wilderness of the western world, its descendants of kings and queens, rich nations of warriors and great priests; kingdoms of Gods and Goddesses, robbed of the powerful ancestral knowledge of our natural powers endowed within us; rightful heirs to sieged thrones and sabotaged nations calculatedly oppressed for more than 400 years. Only a person who is well aware of this would want to keep this information from you in an envious fury that you will become more powerful than them. Let the consciousness of having been deceived make the fire of freedom burn all the more fiercely in your souls.

8

Foreign Drugs—
No Passport Needed

I always had it in my thoughts that the drugs I was selling would provide a better life for me and my family as a way to happiness and success, and for a while it did. The money provided me with an abundance of new clothes and shoes my mother couldn't afford to buy for me in my youth, and I never went hungry because I had money to feed myself. Drug money provided a roof over my head to sleep under, money to pay the bills, and cars to get where I needed to go. In this journey to happiness I also found my misery. The desire to live a better life, void of poor living circumstances, actually destroyed it and made my life miserable. It was all stress and drama. Yeah I had a big ass house that I lived in alone; had five cars and a motorcycle and didn't bring half of them out; a bunch of jewelry that I couldn't wear at the same time; a condo, a townhouse, and two apartments that I only slept in twice; all the champagne and liquor I drank just to piss it out and mess up my insides.

It took for me to go through the highs and lows, toils and tragedy's of the dope game, in all its street star glory near death close call shoot outs, robbery's and kidnappings, police harassments and prison sentences before I realized how drugs were meant to decimate black communities into crack and heroin addicts, to be too distracted from overcoming adversities, and drug laws instituted to remove any street smart drug entrepreneurs not addicted.

The 1980's ushered in the crack epidemic, the worst form of chemical warfare that African American neighborhoods had ever faced. We have never recovered from the psychological and financial drain from neither the drugs nor the war on drugs. The epidemic jumpstarted the Prison Industrial Complex and will affect all generations to come. The racial disparities cant be ignored when blacks are charged and convicted for drug offenses, whites are given less time; part of a settled policy to keep them down, no matter what they do to elevate themselves.

These manufactured and processed drugs from aboard, aided and abetted by U.S. Government agencies to bring into the U.S. to fund wars in other countries and decimate black communities by either addictive means, violent crimes, and incarceration by drug laws under the pose of "War on Drugs" Under the banner of a so-called war on drugs, an assembly line of our sons, uncles, fathers and friends have gone straight into the prison industrial complex. Despite the fact that whites use more illicit drugs than blacks, a cottage prison industry swallowed up hundreds of thousands of black and brown people. By 2002, the U.S. prison population reached an historic 2 million with about half a million of those being drug-related, non-violent offenses.

It should've better been labeled ; "The War on Blacks", how its eroding entire cities and communities, reducing human beings to zombies, residential neighborhoods to war zones, and breakdown society's very fabric to be free of unwanton intrusion upon an individuals liberty. Crack introduction destabilized communities of color. People didn't process the utter bomb dropped on them. The war on drugs has taken millions of American black lives than any war. Blacks have become prisoners of war. Black generations born within the previous several decades aren't given much of a choice in avoiding this drug intrusion ramification one way or another.

Society as a whole is affected directly or indirectly in dealing with a family member lost to drugs. A drug addict looking to score his next hit rob's a victim or kills them for cash or merchandise. A drug dealers gets arrested and citizens of the state pays in taxes to house, clothe, and feed him his entire incarceration stay. Persons convicted of drug offenses who reside locally are ten times more likely to get a harsher prison sentence than someone not of the area, or of the country for that matter. These individuals arrested and convicted more than likely doesn't even own a passport nor has the resources or connections for mass drug importation and trafficking.

These foreign drugs: Cocaine thats made in South America; Heroin thats made in Central America, Afghanistan, and Asia; and Fentanyl thats made in China. I've never been to these countries, nor are any of these drugs produced in any of the United States of America.

Just recently over the previous two decades there's been a wave of concern over prescription drug opioid use and meth—both easily classifiable as white race drugs. Most prescription drugs are manufactured overseas, but meth is dangerously easily to make with most ingredients sold at local convenience stores.

Meth, in all its addictive destruction, can be the new form of crack epidemic, but for the wh te race. The only defeatedness of that scenario is the less likely harsh prison sentences whites would receive compared to blacks caught in possession of the drug. Another additive being the increase of charging for similar drug amounts, where as a black person would be charged for possession with intent to deliver or distribute a controlled substance, or manufacturing and delivery of a controlled substance within a 1,000 feet of a school, church, or park—all of which should have originally just been a possession drug offense

These additives increases the sentencing ranges by double or quadruple it normally would be in range of. I can't close out this chapter without addressing further the addictive dependency society fuels these drug trade markets. In all our modern advances in civilization, we still haven't figured out how to cope without simulation or desensitization and just be. Its coping mechanisms in order to escape our realities, traumas, griefs, and boredom.

Cigarettes, alcohol, Xanax, acid, lean, ecstasy, Molly's, perks, and cannabis aid these addictive methods to reach escape velocity of the mind. One would have to develop an iron constitution of will power to remain sober minded in todays time and still pronounce contentedly with life's perils. Not to confuse my sincerity for people truly struggling with drug addictions in an effort to chase away their mental and emotional demons.

I can admit I too endured with a love one while they battled through past traumas with the assistance of substance abuse, as I watch them destroy themselves daily, and prevented numerous suicide attempts. I only wish I had someone like me there to help me through my own bouts of PTSD, depression and series of emotional turmoil over the years when I sought refuge in alcohol and drug money instead of counseling and God.

Breaking the strongholds of drug addiction is a community effort amongst those who want to see you thrive. Allowing the government to dictate that recovery will result in prison terms. Though prison helped me, it did so in a way to help me finally let go of all I was so desperately trying to keep hold on to. Being that of toxic relationships, a dangerous lifestyle, and overvalued materialistic possessions acquired from drug money.

Prison sentences aren't always the best option; it just furthers the cycles of victimization. Love and assistance would be better than isolation and punishment. Albeit a better recovery program investment only if the U.S. government didn't have other plans to keep its greater hold of citizens on drugs in all due intentions.

9

USA,Inc–
A Free Country Built By Slaves

The U.S. Government does as governments are apt to do–it sides with the rich and powerful as long as it's politically correct to do so regrading abolishment of profited enterprises. So the issue of slavery wasn't so well regarded as an inhuman industry for labor. A hundred years ago men were not at all ashamed of growing rich in this bad way. They were respected in society as much as other men, but not the working men and women.

The very oppressed citizens of this country ancestors that toiled and slavishly built the economical richness that it contains. The American railways, cities, mills, factories, industry plants and warehouses, even building the White House, yet these very descendants are denied access and equality to the structures and lands rightly theirs.

A few men today control all the industries within the U.S. that was obtained by pure thievery, deceit, and barbarism, and can paralyze the economy at their choosing, and the wages of its people depends almost entirely upon the wills of a dozen men. Great industrial organizations of the country controlling everything they used. Greedily monopolizing to own all the oil there is in the United States, and another handful of men owing all the coal, and a few more owning all the iron mines in the U.S. They don't respect the laws because they live above and beyond the laws. Spheres of restrictions that they live outside of but usually have a great hand in creating.

No law was ever by the people; they are made for the people. When these corporate few commit offenses, sometimes totaling billions in criminal net revenue, the courts are silent, and not even so much as a second mention from State's Attorney's, Governors, or the officers of the law. But a black drug dealer in possession of 1 kilo of crack-cocaine with a estimated street value of $30,000 can be charged, convicted, and sentenced to life in prison while a white person charged, convicted of fraud and embezzling billions, damaging the lives of thousands making their lives wrecks, can get off without serving not even so much as a day of jail time shows who the real crooks and criminals are.

These monsters are riding million-dollar jets over the American people. It is the working man who will be guilty of the crimes they create. Only the poor go to jail. It is the wealthy powerful and politically strong who have the keys to the jails and the penitentiaries. Intentions are for the working man, and they're friends, to never have the keys. Their business has been to build them and to fill them.

This blatant disregard for human life because of social status continues further still in being humiliatingly forced to submit to segregation. Laws created may have outlawed this practice but it doesn't stop it from happening.

All aspects of civil society, blacks are still outcasted and perpetually taken advantage of. In housing; blacks are regularly shifted towards communities of African Americans or utterly harassed if living among whites. Forced by restrictions of real estate men and housing project programs into congested rural districts that give rise to vice, crime, and disease because of crowded conditions.

In employment; blacks are routinely looked over for promotions or as new hires, even when abundantly qualified. In education; clandestinely segregated school districts in spite of the law to the contrary, blacks public schools are given less state funding for newer books and learning materials, qualified teachers, overcrowded classroom sizes, and schools built along busy roadways producing massive pollution and are prone to staff strikes every school year.

Now currently the U.S. Government has refused entry to latin immigrants and placed a ban on muslim countries from entering the U.S. A country fully comprised of immigrants to begin with. I believe it's safe to say the U.S. is run and control ed by its creditors, and all politicians are in some form or another just officers of the large corporation, the poor and middle class citizens composed of its stock holdings.

This injustice in the courts will eventually create mass civil unrest, combined with the increasing unemployment and the gap between the rich and the poor.

Resilience through constant generational adversity's of segregation and lynching, poor schools, denial of the right to vote, bad treatment, lack of privileges, and oppression keeps a constant reminder that this way will be a continual show of promotion in the persecution of blacks. Yet this treatment is prejudicial to the interests of all.

Race prejudice has been and will always be the fatal weakness of America. Advocating for equality and liberty by society as a whole is required to reconstruct our government and rebuild our civilization in conformity with the demands of modern efficiency by placing every man, regardless of his color, wherever he may do the greatest good for the greatest number. But when you put profits over people you only stain the future with smears of brutal insolent history.

10

Snitches Without Stitches—
No Honor Among Thieves

Coming through the new prisoner entrance doors at the Metropolitan Corrections Center, downtown Chicago, the posting; "WHY DO TEN WHEN YOU CAN TELL ON A FRIEND!" Will be plastered on the wall for new comer arrestees'. The sight of the sign made me nauseous in my thoughts of the multitude of people who followed that suggestion. To be a part of the criminal culture but turn on your partners in crime as a snitch, is the lowest of labeled life forms. As much as it's common though it should be expected if your committing crimes with someone.Trading against your own brethren is a treasonous act, and todays new age criminals seem more apt to side with the law rather than face their time ahead alone.

Estimates suggest that one in twelve men in urban communities has been used as an informant. One of the many problems with getting "Caught Up"/"Jammed Up" with the law is that one is placed in a compromised position whether they are good for the crime or not.

Sadly, too many will sell their mothers soul to avoid prosecution. It's this custom so readily taken in some instances its become the new normalcy that afterwards they still come around and be celebrated whereas before snitches were in some instances killed for taking the stand, writing statements, and gold fingering targets of investigations.

My pose about the title chapter plays more in the fact of brother going against brother. To have honor is the most respectable virtue aside loyalty to your brother in arms. Sometimes it's too late before you can really recognize the honorable character in the person who you've been dealing with for years until an unprepared situation arises that puts their loyalty and character to the test. Making it essential that you make the correct judgements ahead of time, judging them by their motives, and to judge them by the side they are on.

Perceive clearly its three types of snitches: 1) The kind that commits crimes with people of the like in nature, then when they get arrested turn state witness against their codefendants or life-long friends and people they know for a reduced sentence; 2) Is the kind of regular citizen hater that goes out their way to commit themselves to give information against you as part of their judicial need to fulfill by removing all criminals from society in their phone calls to 911, witness accounts, and grand jury testimonies; 3) Kind is one of a many who has only himself to blame. He is his own snitch by the stupidly signed statements of guilt, interrogation confessions, and many social media posts bragging and displaying his crimes and criminal profits for the world to see, then act on to get charged and convicted.

I included this chapter portion of the book because being Federal indicted by the cause of a snitch, I'm enveloped in the nature of it. Surrounded by gentlemen that qualify as number 1 or number 3, and dutifully affected in some form or fashion by a number 2. Only if these brothers had shut the fuck up sooner, just do your time like a man, like a warrior seized and now prisoner of war. Heaven will avenge your cause.

11

Lynching Mob–
Police & Prosecutors

To understand the Hanging Tree is to understand the noose and the term lynch. Lynching was a very violent act done to blacks; a term that was taken from the name of Col. Charles Lynch who was a land owner in Virginia in 1790. Lynch would hold illegal trials of local lawbreakers in his front yard. Upon conviction of the accused, which was usually the case, Lynch would hang or whip the suspects while they were tied to a tree in his front yard. This became the term referred to as Lynching. But Lynching doesn't only mean hanging. It often included torture by burning, dismemberment, and castration.

Victims were beaten and whipped, many in front of large crowds. Coal tar was used to douse the poor victim prior to setting them on fire. White onlookers would fire rifles and pistols hundreds of times into the corpse while people cheered and children played. Blacks were hacked to death, dragged behind cars, burned, beaten, whipped, mutilated, or shot hundreds of times.

There were a number of offenses that were considered worthy of lynching a black person such as:

- Insulting a white man
- Arguing with a white man
- Improper with a white woman
- Frightening a white woman
- Trying to colonize blacks
- Eloping with a white woman
- Living with a white woman
- Entering a white woman's house
- Peeping Tom looting
- Grave robbing
- Murder
- Kidnapping
- Trying to vote
- Rape
- Using obscene language to a white person demanding respect

This list made blacks available for lynching at any given time. Even if the crime was questionable, vigilante justice by unruly mobs of white people ruled the day. Someone arrested by the police would be abducted by mobs from the jail or courthouse and taken to be lynched before justice has been sought.

Alabama was nicknamed "The Land of Hanging Trees" because there were so many lynchings. Racial terrorism is rich in America, deeply rooted in its soil. Centuries old trees bear the dried blood, mutilated remains and burnt charred bodies of innocent men, pregnant women, little children, and whole families smoldered into its barks, its roots, and leaves.

Lynchings were a method of social and racial control meant to terrorize Black Americans into submission. Old photos depict now white grandfathers and mothers in smiling faces or smug glares of white men, women and children, posing in front of lynched black people dangling from nooses, or standing amid the charred remains of some black father, son, human-being. These white monsters still live on today, unashamed of the horrific acts committed in the past.

Blood thirsty white Lynch mobs of lawyers, policemen, judges, business owners and fellow housewives and school children, partook in the killings of blacks without repercussions. These so-called "Good Christians" murdered, assaulted, raped or injured thousands of innocent black lives.

From an objective point of origin, criminal law does not seem better than the criminals prosecuted. It makes little attempt to mitigate any of the wretchedness that it judges; in many cases it moves only to inflict an additional burden of suffering. The result is tragedy. When the cycle of police abuse that includes both unethical and illegal practices is sanctioned by the very government that is supposed to protect them, what recourse is available to African American citizens? Who do we call for relief from the very public servants our taxes pay to protect us?

Not to minimize violent and predatory individuals who in all intent purposes deserve to be locked away from preying upon society. But one can't ignore a clear indication of white police officers from the outset making hostile and aggressive interactions with colored residents, regardless of whether they suspect them of committing a crime or not. Gun plus white cop equals dead black man. Simple mathematics. It's the color of their skin that they feel gives them free reign to ignore their personal rights under the law, and violate their human rights devised by God.

If I could point to one fundamental problem with policing in America, it is that police kill black people because they are black. And while daily and often extreme violence perpetuated against black people goes beyond police, when residents are killed by cops they are killed by representatives of the state; murdered by those who are empowered to protect and serve the public. An evident conspiracy between police offers and prosecutors to violate the rights of those arrested even when there's clear indication or evidence of police misconduct on behalf of the officers actions, but never an acknowledgement by the criminal justice system.

Documentation of police abuse and prosecutorial misconduct are rife. We are bombarded daily with videos of police brutality. Yet evidence of police raping, stealing and killing citizens is met with justification and resistance. The message is that the system must be protected at all costs—even if it means that the results are mistrust and hate of those we pay to insure the carriage of justice.

What is to be said of a profession in which such obscenities like this are made points of honor, or of institutions in which they are an accepted part of the daily routine? When will we realize that the fact that we can become accustomed to anything, however disgusting at first, makes it necessary for us to examine carefully everything we have become accustomed to?

Long before the so-called war of terrorism which was designed to respond to the September 11 attacks, there was the war on black and brown communities replete with torture and other abuses by law enforcement; such as over-policing with stop and frisk infringements upon privacy; constant police surveillance; police brutality; and constant shootings of unarmed black men without justification or accountability.

The obvious assumption is when whites feel threatened, the outcomes for black people are not good. The unwelcoming reception by whites towards blacks can be downright vicious Nothing short of neighborhood terrorists. Innocent blacks, attacked at first for purposes of sport and later for sinister designs, were often badly beaten in the streets, or even murdered. The offenders were not punished and if blacks defended themselves they were usually severely penalized. Treated by prosecutors as numbers not human lives.

The current rate of police killings of Black Americans is nearly the same as the rate of lynchings in the early decades of the 20th Century. Because I'm black, this means I'm five times more likely to be killed by police than my white counterpart. In era's of "No Justice No Peace";"Black Lives Matter"; and "Wake Up Or Sleep Forever", an abundant practice of hunting styled policing, laced with aggressive racial profiling and hostile arrests, still occurs everyday of the week in black and brown communities.

In the late 18th and early parts of the 19th Century, the south, moreover adopted the policy of a more general intimidation of blacks to keep them down. The lynching of blacks for almost any offense, but for whites greatest excuse: assaults on white women was rapidly developed as an institution. Within half the century, more than 4,000 blacks were barbarically burned publicly in the daytime to attract crowds of whites as spectators. Many culprits often often discovered to be white police officers and politicians of these communities taking part in these crimes never to be brought before justice.

As a black person, even when crimes of whites against blacks are finally arrested and charged, the judges are not on your side. They don't look at things the way you do. They are trained and groomed from birth differently. The law in of itself are all the time fashioned against you. Prosecutors have so much influence over grand juries that they could get them to indict a ham sandwich. Grand juries operate more often as the prosecutors pawn than the citizens shield.

Grand juries have become a mockery of a judicial system built on a system of class and race privilege. Nothing just or true or fair will come out of them. This instrument is a left over from a southern aristocracy and have no value in the 21st Century. Ending the Grand Jury system is a legit demand.

additionally, judges will systematically not allow black jurors to serve in criminal case trials when a black defendant is on trial. An apparent tendency toward further segregation. A many time over the police do effect many smart and good plucky captures. Sometimes they are aided by a stupid oversight on the part of the criminal, but quite as often by some extraordinary piece of luck. Majority inner city criminal non-violent crimes arrests arise from harassing racial profiling. A regular interaction I know of all too well being a resident of Chicago's Southside.

Every black man carries with them the anxieties brought on by interactions with white police officers and the inevitable uncle tom house nigger black officers; the kind of brainwashed pathetic black officers that aid the racist white man in his deplorable actions. Tactical police officers would randomly stop you on the street, grabbing you up, turning your pockets inside out, violating your personal privacy with invasive, near to sexual assault, public strip and cavity searches, irrespective of any legal constitutional rights you have. To object to these obtrusive methods would surely land you in jail or the hospital, or both on bogus trumped up false charges.

Most complaints and lawsuits against these violations only increase the intensity in which it happens afterwards. One must ask where did all those hidden faces behind the white sheets go? If you're black, the obvious answer is they now wear a badge, or a black robe still dragging us off, beaten and bloody, to the hanging tree.

12

Slave Ship–Jail Process

The most shocking cruelties were habitually practiced centuries earlier. Poor creatures stolen from their homes packed close, like bales of goods, in the dark holds of ships, nakedly where they were half choked bad odors from accumulated filth, and where they could hardly breathe for want of air. The food allotted them was merely enough to keep them alive. Many died of grief and despair, and still more of burning fevers and other diseases on the forced trike to America. The living and dead often remained huddled together for days and weeks, and when the corpse were removed they were thrown out to the sharks in the Atlantic ocean.

Upon arrival to the Americas and coastal islands, new slaves were branded with hot steel iron on there breast bone with the name of their purchaser. Today's jail inmates being processed into the County Jail are inked marked with their jail I.D. number and classification on there arms and hands, afterwards of being packed into bullpen cells, shoulder to shoulder, of more than a hundred of bodies.

Stuffy defile nauseating orders of stale vomit, feces, feet and days old unwashed body odor consuming what little air present. A dehumanizing experience by all accounts. Left to stand, or lay on the floor in between squeezed bodies with minimum ventilation. Prisoners waiting in the holding tank, w th its dirty floor, its greasy walls, and its vile atmosphere. The sanitary arrangements disgusting. Wooden benches attached to the walls provided the only seats. In this room, old and young. pure and impure, clean and verminous, sane and insane, await their turn to see the bond court judge.

A combination of murderers, rapists, thieves, drunkards, dope sick drug addicts, and dealers. Cash bails required to retain freedom again for already poor people living below the poverty lines. These people already living paycheck to paycheck will lose everything if they can't reach the bail amounts, and be ushered to further humiliation by lined strip searches along the jails tunnel corridor. A hundred naked bodies next to one another at the dehumanizing orders of Cook County Sheriff guards. Brutal assaults ensued if demands aren't carefully followed.

It's here, majority of felony cases won't progress to any significant conclusions for months, and in some cases years. No wonder the jails and prisons are overcrowded. Cases that timely investigations into the defendants defense won't commence until days before trial; Almost always years after the initial arrest has taken place, hurting leads, potential witnesses, and the defendants morality to prove his innocence.

The jails conditions of confinement adds to the decrease of morality. Sleeping in the presence of rats and roaches infestations; poor lighting and ventilation; gang fights and predatory inmates; abusive correctional officers and health deteriorating food makes all the matters worst. It stands to the credit of our penal system that it is much easier for a guilty man to escape than it is for an innocent man to be punished. The negative affects upon the purest of minds are endless, for the prisoner and his family of loved ones suffering because of his absence. At no time during the history of the penal system has it shown that solitude and severity has proven effectual for reformation; its deadening and soul-destroying. It brings one face to face with suffering and comparable death. Make death long delayed in suffering, waiting, hoping for the end, all alone in the world. Just to wait and hope for the end.

Idle liberty is dangerous to young men who have no desire for wrong-doing, but who at the same time have little aspiration for right-doing. Our prisons are crowded with them, and a series of short imprisonments only serves to harden them, until they become confirmed criminals. The purest example being incarcerated juveniles almost always go on to be later imprisoned as adults.

The making of a habitual criminal, sin-seared, oft-convicted, hardened by his struggles, of whom there are no hope; classified as a danger to the community and a pest to society, well known to the prison system—now a hopeless, dead alive man. Tempered by pity circumstances being against them.

These under guided, underfed and under provided for, of little intelligence, with no moral consciousness, they are a by product of our civilization, a direct product of our slum life.

Had they been caught while young and given years of manual ethics training, vocational education, nutritious meals, together with manly examples to live up to, many would be provided a reasonable start in life. Given a different outcome of life. But in many instances of real old criminals, after committing crimes, will be sentenced to a few months or a year or so, but many years in prison sentenced for a young man of his twenties, a first offender.

Centuries earlier, young slaves were worth more than old ones, enabling the slavers to make more money from the more use of their youthful time span. The slaves age, now modern young inmate, provides a new account number to make money from, compared to the older criminal, already a settled permeant account, set to make returns to the prison system until their death—closing the account.

This business doesn't acknowledge forgiveness. Having sympathy isn't part of the sentencing judges design, just as much as it isn't for slave-traders over the cries, pleads, tears, and appeals for mercy from the slave. The pleas for mercy by a prisoner before the judge generally have an opposite effect to that he wishes. The economics of the profit to loss in this industry dictates almost certainty the length of sentences given. This ship is permanently set to sail in this manner.

13

Modern Day Slavery–
Billion Dollar Industry

If the average life span of a human being were a 100 years old, that would mean just four of my ancestors earlier were part of the 40 million men, women, and children kidnapped from their native land of West Africa. 4 million Native American men, women, and children kidnapped and sent abroad. Today, 4 million black, brown men, women, and children introduced to the new slavery method through incarceration within' the United States prison systems by coded laws, ownership of life insurance policies by unaware voluntary means through registered social security numbers, birth certificates, and drivers licenses.

Over two million people are in U.S. prisons, the highest number of any developed country in the world. Black men are over-represented in the prison industrial complex–the genesis of their incarceration can be traced back to disproportionate suspension rates in school, disproportionate interactions with police, and disproportionate rates of convictions along with harsher and longer sentences. The cycles continues and the perception of dangerous black men becomes an entrenched American reality.

The mainstream media is always happy to lend a helping hand in the criminalization of African Americans, blacks are 75 percent more likely than whites to be stopped by cops, almost twice as likely than their white counterparts to be searched and less likely for the search to result in the discovery of contraband. Yet we keep filing up the jails and prisons, thanks in a large part to racist policies such as mandatory sentencing and three strikes.

Over the past century, the criminal justice system has been used as a method of municipal income stream by the intentional use of racial profiling to shake down working class black residents for minor violations as a collection agency to bring in city revenue, and with the poor designed to be the product goods. Blacks folks are also the targets of constant, dangerous levels of criminalization; from the schoolhouse and place of worship to the worksite, and from pool parties to the evening news. The department of justice has found nearly every major city in America police and courts guilty of widespread abuse, racial profiling, and brutal misconduct targeting black residents.

African Americans are disproportionately represented at nearly every stage of law enforcement, from the initial police contact to final disposition of a case in municipal court. Black people are also used as law enforcement's ATM–excessively ticketed for minor offenses, arrested and unjustly imprisoned if they can not afford bail.

The early 1920's Great Depression resulting in the United States supplementing its national creditor debt with insurance policies upon unsuspecting American citizens. The century earlier loss of free slave labor would be converted into prisoner labor to recognize the slavery abolishment laws set in by the U.S. Constitution. But the abolishment of slavery didn't come full circle immediately. The plan of emancipation was adopted gradually, slaves under the new name of apprentices, were obliged to work for their masters six years longer without wages, except one day and a half in the week. All children six years old were unconditionally free, and no human being could be sold; but the masters being, deprived of the power to sell the children, they refused to supply them with any food. In fact, they contrived every way to make black people think they had better lives had they remained slaves.

On June 19,1865, two and a half years after the emancipation proclamation and almost two months after the end of the Civil War, slaves in the furthest slave state of Texas were declared free, but slavery took on a new fascist method in the form of the criminal justice system.

The 13th Amendment to the constitution, which is commonly thought to codify the elimination of slavery, has this clause: "Neither slavery nor involuntary servitude, except as a punishment for crime whereof the party shall have been duly convicted, shall exist within the United States, or any place subject to their jurisdiction."

During the Jim Crow era, this exception in the 13th Amendment was used to re-enslave as many as 1 million African Americans in the south. Charging them with various petty crimes to be forced into unpaid labor as the sentence. This labor befitted various contracted out businesses in making consumer products. This practice still goes on in America today. As many as five states have inmates working with no pay. Many of them work for private sector manufactures and retailers, making consumer products that many of us unknowingly purchase. Even for those who are paid, the daily wages can amount to pennies per hour worked.

Even as still now, the improvements of blacks into middle class living standards, are subjected to the prison system which has only benefitted the rich and wealthy who don't pay taxes at the expenses of the poor confined and faced with the harsh realities that the middle class ignorantly support, finance, and oversee its daily operations, much akin to slavers–slave holder masters–slaves held in bondage. It's this transition easily parallel to today's criminal justice system: poor person inmate (slave)–judge (slave holder master)–police (slavers).

A time warp of oppression and the oppressed, this broker justice system is ambiguous with large factory prisons to produce goods and services at nearly free labor costs provided by kidnapped souls from the slums of Americas city streets. Whole communities of fatherless children, bound by circumstances to repeat at the same cycles of drugs, violences, prison, and death. Conditions set to abuse, maltreat, and socially despise blacks who in the eyes of white men had no rights that should be respected on the basis that the African Negro had no chance for racial development in this country.

In they're plan they could secure no kind of honorable employment, could not associate with congenial white friends whose minds and pursuits might operate as a stimulus upon their industry, and could not rise to the level of the successful professional or businessmen found around them.

The progress of blacks in America was much more marked after the middle of the Nineteenth Century. But this progress would have to be contained and limited to a few who managed to escape the slums, wars, and brutal efforts to be placed in the prison system by racially charged police officers intended to wrangle up as many of the poor and middle-class blacks to aid to this system. The poor class is paid for by the middle class to profit the wealthy and rich classes of society.

Courts operating as institutions, and not persons; the lawyers are the stock-brokers, prisons and jails are the individual stock holding companies, and you are the stock if incarcerated under this system.

A diabolical scheme to ensure a oppressed life path from the outset: slave to hardworking industrious employee supporting a poor family; onward to successfully middle-class standard living of a decent home and community; usher in drugs, and alcohol, economic stalemate and crime, disease and malicious persecutions to eliminate any hope for prosperity and recovery. Now a return arrival back to slave status, comparable to quicksand: the more you claw your way out; the deeper you sink in.

14

Penitentiary Deliverers—
Public Defenders

Justice delayed is justice denied. At arrival in the criminal justice system, if you can't afford a private attorney than one will be provided for at no monetary costs. But the unforeseen costs will ultimately lead to your demise in some unfortunate form or another. These defenseless defense attorney's providing no defense at all, will shoe you along and in most incidents keep pertinent discovery information from you that can prove your innocence. Attorney's that tell lies in court and judges who ignore it. Prosecutors conspire with public defenders to violate your rights and maintain oppression over your misery until you give in.

Even hiring a private attorney doesn't guarantee you justice but it does give you a fighting chance—depending upon how long your money is. In this regular practice, there's a reasonable expectation that a person getting a paycheck from the same person that arrested you, that's prosecuting you, and that'll be judging whether your guilt or innocence, is all in cahoots together. You're the only one ignorant of the game ploy being played against you.

These government positions may have the impression of just a job as a civil servant for the judge, prosecutor, court room employees, and police officers, but it's your life that rests vulnerably in their hands. It's a terrifying feeling of a violation being committed against you, but utterly powerless to defend against and helpless in protecting yourself from.

While the intellectual and legal battle is as bitter as any physical one. To the understanding observer and the participant it is momentous and intense. Essentially they are at war; otherwise they would not be in court. The only reason for their being there is an issue to be decided: your guilt or innocence; freedom or imprisonment. The lawyer must be adamantly ready to fight, bite, scratch, shoot, kill, slash for your cause. As an officer of the court he is sworn to promote justice; as a champion in the battle he is under the deep obligation of performing his utmost for his client. This is suppose to be the hired or assigned attorneys job to do.

Additionally, the lawyers are primarily in court to please their clients. Every ruling of the judge against them on even minor points of evidence, any adverse decision is fatal to them from the point of view of retaining the client for the next litigation.

The lawyer must be vigilant from the beginning of the trial to the end. If anything of significance escapes his notice he may lose his whole case, and at your expense.

Any lawyer knows how important the pleadings are, but nobody else does. The judge does not pay any more attention to them than he has to. Juries hardly ever see them; if they did, they could not understand them.

The witnesses never hear of them, the clients have sworn they have read them and have sworn that they are true. Yet not one client in a thousand could give an explanation of them other than; "My lawyer told me to sign it, so I did". This cop a plea quickly method is heavily favored among all public defenders for the reduced work load commitment to it that it' l provide even though they're suppose to do everything private lawyers do: be with you at your hearings as your voice of representation; go through evidence of your case with you; investigate that evidence in your case to see if the police and prosecutor are lying or what they accuse you of is true to be proven undoubtably; negotiate plea deals; and represent you at trial.

But being buried in criminal cases while working 60-70 hours a week, its not possible to ethnically represent appointed clients. The people are not treated as human beings but as just another case file. Cases to whom which they haven't the slightest clue on how to proceed on or bulk of evidence used against the persons accused of crimes not reviewed. Carrying more than hundreds of cases at a time, an obvious attention to detail deficient is abundant.

A now national epidemic crises of over-worked and underpaid public defenders along with mandatory minimum sentences, grinds the entire justice system to a halt. It doesn't fund a legitimate defense while it continues to lock up everyone. Too many cases, not enough funding provided for more hired attorneys to represent clients which keeps them in jail longer, conviction rates higher.

Just more overcrowded jails and prisons, more delays, no justice provided. Guidelines mandate they are suppose to abide by to not take on more cases than they can handle. This is to limit the risk of under misrepresentation of legal counsel. remember, "If you can't afford an attorney then one will be provided for you'… At the further cost of your life and freedom. These public defenders aka penitentiary deliverers handle as much as 95% of the criminal cases in the major cities across America. Of the 80% in these cases people being blacks.

There aren't enough public defenders to get to cases, leaving men, women, and children to remain incarcerated for weeks, months, and years pending the outcome of their case. Too poor to post bail, and no home, no property holdings for collateral. A wide-spread problem across the country that prays into the favor of the wealthy prison system benefactors. All the more making for a fundamental distrust of justice itself. Those seeking closure will find resentment instead against the courts technicalities of procedure with its long and fatal delays of the law.

In my own experiences sometimes the best bet was to have saved my money and allowed a public defender to defend my criminal case because of the relationship with the judge and prosecutor for a fair plea deal. Other times it proved fatal for my defense. The public defender took months just to look over my case while I sat away in jail, then upon the first meeting just before court told me only what plea deal she could get me. Going to trial was never discussed as an option even when evidently innocent.

Contrary to the very notion: Presumed guilty until you can prove your innocence. Today's issues of prison reform can't be properly addressed without correcting this tragic inception for the ones suffering daily from this expediency of injustice. The rich don't apply in this chapter. The scales of justice are forever tipped in their favor. The apparent mass inequality where there is a law for the poor man and another law for the rich. The high-priced millionaire escapes and the low-slummed shop lifter goes to prison.

On a closer required review, a rich man caught in gigantic scheme for defrauding the government of millions of dollars is only fined, whereas the poor thief caught stealing groceries is sent to jail. Or take the high financier who wrecks the lives of thousands into bankruptcy and serves a light prison sentence and emerges from his prison term still rich. But the peddler on the Southside who sells a few bags of dope worth $20 is punished to the full limit of the law.

The facts exist and is not hard to find. There is undoubtedly a miscarriage of judging and of justice, as though there was an unwritten law in the back of the human mind in favor of the wealth classes. The high-powered attorney for the rich with the refutable reputation comes into court for his client above any impressions of being the usual subservient and cringing, but confidently fierce, humorous and polite. Almost always he is a friend or close associate to the judge. It's an open and close shut victory for the wealthy, never to be a player on the board game, but instead the games developer.

15

Deaf, Dumb & Blind–
Ignorance Of Rights

Fredrick Douglass once said; "Find out just what any people will quietly submit to and you have the exact measure of the injustice and wrong which be imposed on them. The worst part of being deaf, dumb and blind is being told to be so. For some it's a comparatively easy matter, but for others it's not only more difficult, but expensive, and at times dangerous. 99% of the people arrested don't know their legal rights, nor the procedure code of laws broken they stand accused of.

School lesson plans teach you the constitution but don't teach you how it apply's to your everyday life; Money, Love, Law are essential lessons in life that need to be taught in all stages of education. Poor blacks and latinos are grossly ignorant of the law and of their individual rights. But as the law states: "Ignorance of the law is not an excuse". Sadly most people allow themselves to be ruled and guided by the opinion of others, especially in the legal context.

Public defenders and even some paid lawyers will put so much fear behind a felony charge to scare an innocent defendant into a guilty plea; whereby the proof of guilt is abandoned and substituted for persuasion and heresay. The results are both grotesque and pitiful. Presenting another evil ploy level set out against the poor defendant by stacking criminal convictions for later use against him to increase new arrest charges for harsher prison sentence terms. It's the idea presented that the whole criminal case ordeal can be over with quickly if you just take the plea.

The hard fought other option for setting and holding trial takes months, and the likelihood of winning is a coin toss in most instances depending on the skills of hired counsel and evidence against you.

In all, we suffer at times from the common illusion that the problems of today are entirely new; we fancy that nobody ever thought of them before, and that when we have solved them, nobody will ever need to look for another solution.

In this mistake of thinking, viewing the United States Bill of Rights ten original Amendments to the Constitution, and how its respected by civl service members in today's actual life contexts situations:

1) Congress shall make no law respecting an establishment of religion, or prohibiting the free exercise thereof; or abridging the freedom of speech, or of the press, or the right of the people peaceably to assemble, and to petition the government for a redress of grievances;

2) A well-regulated militia, being necessary to the security of a free state, the right of the people to keep and bear arms, shall not be infringed;

3) No soldier shall, in time of peace be quartered in any house, without the consent of the owner, nor in time of war, but in a manner to be prescribed by law;

4) The right of the people to be secure in their persons, houses, papers, and effects, against unreasonable searches and seizures, shall not be violated, and no warrants shall issue, but upon probable cause, supported by oath or affirmation, and particularly describing the place to be searched, and the persons or things to be seized;

5) No person shall be held to answer for a capital, or otherwise infamous crime, unless on a presentment or indictment of a grand jury, except in cases arising in the land or naval forces, or in the militia, when in actual service in time of war or public danger; nor shall any person be subject for the same offense to be twice put in jeopardy of life or limb; nor shall be compelled in any criminal case to be a witness against himself, nor be deprived of life, liberty, or property, without due process of law; nor shall private property be taken for public use without just compensation;

6) In all criminal prosecutions, the accused shall enjoy the right to a speedy and public trial, by an impartial jury of the state and district wherein the crime shall have been committed, which district shall have been previously ascertained by law, and to be informed of the nature and cause of the accusation; to be confronted with the witnesses against him; to have compulsory process for obtaining witnesses in his favor, and to have the assistance of counsel for his defense;

7) In suits at common law, where the value in controversy shall exceed twenty dollars, the right of trial by jury shall be preserved, and no fact triec by a jury shall be otherwise re-examined in any court of the United States, than according to the rules of the common law;

8) Excessive bail shall not be required nor excessive fines imposed, nor cruel and unusual punishment inflicted;

9) The enumeration in the constitution, of certain rights, shall not be construed to deny or disparage others retained by the people;

10) The powers not delegated to the United States by the corstitution, nor prohibited by it to the states, are reserved to the states respectively, or to the people.

Now if you've learned these bill of rights in grade school just as I have, it was only introducec as a means of remembering to be tested on later, not how it applies or runs painfully contrary to your life experiences ahead. Contrary examples to these rights should have been taught in grade school as well so the youth could have been better prepared to prevent these happenings from occurring or to develop laws to counter them.

In bill 1), an actual infringement does occur. Police set out investigations into rap artists music and works of free expression all the time. Black lives matters supporters are at the helm of federal inquiries equally parallel to the black panther party members of the 1960's ard 70's. Muslim religion followers are categorically stigmatized as terrorists as well as entire muslim religion countries placed on travel bans to the U.S. Numerous assembled peaceful protestors over the decades have been assaulted by police and arrested for exercising this supposed right.

Bill 2) is probably the most dangerous violation committed against the poor. The purposeful disarming of citizens and systemic categorizing of citizens as felons to make them unable to bear arms or placed in prison if they do. It is in this manner the government can take possession of you, your family, and property easily when the economic bubble bursts, and they haul you off to intermediate work camps to toil away for your country for free in its wars against other poor nations; subconsciously disarming the public for preventing protection when society uprising occurs against the wealthy by the poor and middle-class.

Bill 3), in cases of National Guard deployments of its soldiers your rights as a citizen, or a human-being, won't be recognized. Police officers and government agents hardly ever respect homeowner quarters in pursuing suspects or investigations.

Bill 4), the most violated right of all amendments so heavily infringed upon. It's also the only remedy a defendant can claim to reduce injury against his liberty. As a many countless criminal cases or undocumented cases of police performing warrantless searches of homes, cars, offices, and persons.

Falsified warrants laced with perjurer statements by police officers just to secure the warrant by a magistrate judge. Cellular phones tapped and GPS triangulated, and contents observed without owners consent. Drivers vehicles pulled over and obtrusively searched after being racially profiled. Doors of homes battered in on the false pretense of crimes committed, and valuables taken. It's this amendment that citizens are able to use frequently as a recourse in civil court by lawsuits as well for false arrests, violations of the right to be free from illegal search and seizures.

The courts take steps further to reduce your rights by giving the police more leverage by utilizing subterfuge reasons like traffic violations as a reason to search a vehicle; or the smell of cannabis; or its a high-crime area; and their favored: "He fit the description"–young and black.

Bill 5), the modern criminal justice system is seemingly the total opposite of these statements of rights. Grand Jury indictments are presented to closed door sessions of people without the defense nor the presence of the defendants attorney. In these closed hearings everything just shy of making the person accused out to be a terroristic evil monster will be said against them in efforts to secure an indictment against them. If you're convicted of offenses or arrested, or not even of the same as a current charge, you still will be additionally subjected to double jeopardy standard discriminatory practices. Some quadrupled jeopardy for previous arrests, or sentences already served prison time for. Now increased mandatory minimum sentences and extended offense term categorizations that get harsher by the decade will apply.

Moreover, the law may state you shouldn't be compelled to be a witness against yourself, but in the eyes of public opinion, most juries will use this action against you depending on the charisma in your character, softness in your demeanor, and any flaws in your appearance. Yet the likelihood of the weight of evidence against you determining the outcome as guilt or innocence is unlikely. It's the presented presumption.

Bill 6), the obvious un-enjoyment process of a criminal case as I've stated before is grossly delayed. If the defense files pre-trial motions, sometimes they could run for a year and a half before being heard. A jury with black citizens are excluded almost immediately if the defendant is black or a white defendant is on trial for a crime against a black person. And the provided assistance of counsel for defense could prove fatal under the penitentiary deliverer standards.

Bill 7), other than suits, another important matter should be addressed about the difficulties of where the unknown mostly occur because if we were to be held in jurisdiction under the common law, all these enacted U.S. codes wouldn't exist. Crimes for traffic offenses, drugs, guns and all else doesn't exist under common law; only crimes against persons and property. It is by the unknowingly voluntary induction means that we, the poor and middle-class, allow ourselves to be subjected to these coded laws. The common law is the original law of man. The U.S. Government has contrived these coded laws for protection of its economic interests, not the safety protection of its citizens.

Bill 8), in the fall of 2013, I was arrested for drug possession. A low amount of crack-cocaine, and going before the judge for a bail, and was given a $250,000 cash bail amount order. It was an excessive bail amount in comparison to the inmates charged for murder, attempted murder, robberies, and various other violent crimes whose bail amounts were less than mine.

What constitutes cruel and unusual punishment? Could it be the forced incarceration until the conclusion of your criminal case by a coerced plea deal? Is it the malnutrition jail meals, squalid living conditions amongst rats and roaches, freezing ventilation temperatures, abusive jail guards, lack of fresh air and sunlight, dehumanizing strip searches and brutal staff assaults? Solitary confinement that breaks down mental and emotional normal standards w th forth-coming new disorders. Are these excessive unlawful conditions of confinement qualified as cruel and unusual? Because there all the current jail and prison circumstances.

Bill 9), its very existence anc construction is ignored and not construed in any context to accept rights except on appeal and presentation.

Bill 10), it is the people disparaged systematically. The public at large are controlled by delegated United States politicians totally out of tune with the people whom they are suppose to represent. Instead they represent their wealthy financial sponsors to enact causes to their benefits.

All in all it is better to know these facts and not need them then to need them and not know them. personally, the more I learned, i became addicted to the new euphoria of knowledge, wisdom, and understanding. Educating myself in all forums of criminal and civil law, history, and business, literature, science and technology, philosophy and medicine, economics and politics. The goal wasn't to know everything, but a little about a lot. The ignorance could cost your life to this corrupt system if one doesn't know how to navigate it well.

16

Time Not For Crime–
Unnecessary Extended Sentences

At this current mass incarceration stage, if you've been convicted of prior crimes and are arrested for a new crime, even if innocent, charges will be enhanced to mandatory minimums far exceeding the original charge statues. In all effects, you'll be doing additional time for a crime you've already done time for. Many police officers and prosecutors already know this before pursuing investigations, and will direct their investigations to cater to maximizing your sentencing ranges.

It's not my belief that the founding fathers of the constitution and this nation had any intentions for the early laws it got from England to be later construed in this manner.

The original criminal law dealt only with crimes of violence, such as murder, rape, and assault. Now that the U.S. has been corporated, its swayed its laws to the benefits of the company, even at the costs of human life and liberty. It's this corrupt objective that begets problems in civilization, religion, law, and convention. The constant attempts made by the wills of individuals and classes to thwart the wills and enslave the powers of other individuals and classes.

Lawmakers and the judge, become instruments of tyranny in the hands of those who are too narrow-minded to understand law and exercise judgement; and in their hands law becomes tyranny, totally ignorant of the prison sentences that destroys families; ravish communities in purging them of effective leaders, and breeding grounds for unguided youth to subscribe to the ills of idle thinking and persuasive negative actions into criminal activities.

Things worsen evermore with mandatory minimums for non-violent drug crimes by over-zealous officers and prosecutors to obtain career markers with conviction counts. These coercion styled obtained convictions and sentences by jailing a poor classed individual unable to meet cash bail amounts festers into desperation to salvage their family and possessions, and only hopes of saving yourself, and your life, is to confess to crimes accused of to return back to the life left behind as quickly as possible.

This corrupt criminal justice system that all too often persecutes people who did nothing wrong, who over-sentence people, show no mercy, and who are in positions that have no accountability. Many non-violent offenders are hit with sentences that are way longer than those given to violent offenders and sex offenders who actually caused great physical and emotional harm to their victims. And many other people in prison are serving harsh penalties for minor, non-violent crimes. The vast majority of these inmates being people of color.

The police have even made it a point of coming after our arts and music. Free expression will and can be used against you to persuade your judge and jury to convict you and impose harsher sentences. You will be made guilty according to your habits, not judged guilty or innocent according to your acts. Rather his vices made him guilty, his virtues does not make him innocent, but the individual should be allowed not to have been pre-judged off his culture. Nor should an individual be punished continuously for a crime he already served the sufficient sentence term for.

The courts make the further mistake of not recognizing an economically struggling person just as parallel to an individual struggling or handicapped with drug or substance abuse addictions. There's a need to institute programs to cater and aid these persons driven to crime as a means to acquire monetary means for shelter, food and clothing. Time is our most precious commodity and cannot be recovered once lost or taken away. To punish harshly persons not normally given to criminal activity, if the circumstances had not induced it, is cruel and unusual punishment.

When the state finds in its jails and prisons a number of people who are constantly committing offenses, who are helpless and penniless, and whose mental or economical condition is so low that they are not fit to be detained in prison, provisions should be made for their being permanently established resources.

moreover, prison reform needs to drastically began at the level of lobbied laws to reverse this oppressive criminal justice system intentions to create permanent prisoner residents.

17

State Tree vs. Federal Tree-
State Prison & Federal Prison

There are three things peculiarly essential to health: plenty of clean water to drink; plenty of fresh air to breath; and enough of nourishing food to eat. All these are luxury's in jail and prison to obtain. Health deteriorating food consumed that'll usher in long-term health deficiency diseases, lower libidos, inhibit reproduction ability, and hazardous ingredient substances that'll grow breast in men. In these forced squalid conditions daily, they expect you to return to society normal or better still—reformed.

Its here the daily suffering breaks the mental and emotiona solitude barrier. Subjected to cold air temperatures, cold and sparse supply of food, grossly inflated expensive luxuries of phone calls and commissary, which at best is the same food contents sold at gas stations. Hostile attitudes of prisoners bounce off one another in the close living quarters. The smallest spark of an altercation could be the fuse to start a fight, stabbing, or killing.

Endless sounds and countless noises fill every waking moment. Radios, tv's, count times, pointless arguments, keys, cell doors slamming, constant inmates conversations holding no value. So much idleness and worthlessness of a despicable daily routine. But prison offers the time to become disciplined, patient, and self-aware. No one ought to live in idleness, which is the cause of all sorts of discord and trouble.

It took me awhile for me to accept my prison term. I was already three years into a four and a half years would be sentence of 9 years, served at 50%. The prison term allowed me to use focused exercise on my brain with all its mental muscles to increase development, but it took severe mental solitude and fortification to block out all the distractions around me constantly going on, deafening my inner voice, barely able to discern my own thoughts. Support gradually diminished away, until there was barely a person I could call within a year that would answer my phone calls or visit me. With just enough food to keep me alive—merely a little meal daily; my resolve helped me push through the most miserable winters.

When the walls sparkled with frost, and the floor was slippery with ice. Being thin as a skeleton; but still did not die. The outside world has no idea of the horrid circumstances connected with the penal system unless they've been through it. The corrections officer being a witness and parallel prisoner. Just as you cannot imprison a man without imprisoning a warder and C.O. being tied to the prison as effectually by the fear of unemployment and starvation as the prisoner is by the bricks, bolts and bars.

Privately owned prisons make incentives for lawmakers to fill their prisons with people. This transitions to the courts to play by pay along. By all accounts the justice system at the state level would readily give you the plea deal that'll put you back on the streets near freedom the quickest; letting you keep stacking up convictions, preparing you for the ultimate blow: a forceable felony life sentence term by three strikes eligibility.

At the state court level, they'll reduce the charges to almost near no prison time with the right attorney representation. At the federal court level, sentencing guidelines expose defendants to harsh minimum sentencing and life committed to prison maximums if trial verdicts are rendered guilty. All time federally is 85% of term to be served. Plea deals make up the 98% bulk of federal convictions because the evidence against most defendants are so damaging, it would prove of little use and suicidal to go to trial.

Additionally, prosecutors are allowed wide latitude to include damaging hearsay evidence in criminal cases. For instances, a defendant charged with gun possession tries for bond hearing; the prosecutor will put on display in open court any social media photos or videos that has the defendant in any negative compromising states, whether its holding guns or music videos discussing committing violent acts. The defendant is surely to have his bail requests denied. At trial and sentencing, defendants are slandered even worse to taint their image before the judge and jury.

The federal criminal system far exceeds he level of racism at the state criminal system level. Judges are appointed that's been serving on the bench since the civil rights were insulated. These same judges have handed down over a million years in sentences, even for non-violent crimes. Crime bills that reenacted the death penalty, and have race group focused disastrous effects on the people. It's these seeds of hate that grows deep roots of oppression and flourishes flowers of crime and punishment—and more punishment.

18

Abandoned Ship—Left For Dead

Abandonment is an unforgettable injury that forever stains the heart and mind of its victim. It makes a person question what true loyalty is, and the answer comes back that it's a myth. In prosperity and sunshine you find yourself surrounded by flatterers and so-called friends, but let the waves of adversity beat about and threaten to engulf you, then stretch forth your hands for friends you have known and you will find yourself stranded and alone. There may be a few timid, cautious people who feel they would like to give help, but popular opinion and example prove too much for weak natures and it is but charity to let them go. It would take an iron constitution of unconditional love, loyalty, and respect for faithful support to withstand the severe deprivations usually accustomed to.

I put my life on the line selling drugs and hustling work endless hours in the streets to take care of a family that benefitted from it more than me then left me when I got locked up. Gave my blood, sweat, and tears, and all I wanted in return was love, support, and kindness the most, and didn't receive it. Hearts wasn't softened by my misfortunes. It took this moment to realize how much loyalty and trust is hard to find virtues in people.

Being back at the bottom clearly showed who was all down for me unconditionally, and my conditions would require all the support I could muster up. But as the days turned into weeks, and the weeks into months, months into years, the pains of isolation and desertion grew ever intensely along with resentment; Left to bid with my own troubles and challenges.

My first incarceration was a disheartening experience of not receiving the family and friends support I expected. I grew bitterly resentful. Hurt by a love one and abandoned while incarcerated will obsess the painful degree a thousand fold. I can contribute a broken heart for breaking the seal of knowledge, wisdom, and deep understanding that I came into. It was my utter ignorance of women that blinded my hurt ego to see a burning injustice that a woman should suffer so bitterly for a thing which at the time seemed so natural and inevitable as not to be unfaithful and leave a relationship behind without reason

I have witnessed plenty of men broken apart at the seams over their women leaving them. The begging, crying, and yelling over the collect phone calls and visiting rooms. Personally, my own lady leaving me broke my spirit. It was a hard fight to let my reality win and show me what I was failing to see.

How they act when you aren't up will tell a lot about them. The random arguments about pointless old issues, decreasing visitations and unanswered phone calls foretold all I needed to know.

In a modern world where people keep there cellphones with them constantly, whether in the bathroom, sleeping, there shouldn't be an excuse of missing a phone call. It's more like a blatant ignore, and intentions not to answer. So for me, it's a sign that they never really gave a fuck about you in the first place. Love wasn't there enough to answer my call regardless of what I had to say, whether it was to their benefit or not. People moved on without a closure to me, so I needed to learn to move on too.

My return to the streets and my children fueled my hopes. I couldn't afford to think I can't get out because it'll require giving up hope. And as far as the lady that left me, I let go too. Eventually her fatal desires for excitement and not responsibility primarily caused her undoing. It was a painful lesson learned. I shall instruct my son to be sure to marry a woman who has got her wild oats safely over, or select a wife of the more old-fashioned type who does not require them.

The experience of being left behind when I needed help the most killed me internally, and I felt I had died but was still left here on earth to witness all living around but I couldn't talk to, touch, or get to but only to notice and observe from my jail cell window. It ultimately made me question if I died what my life would matter to the people I devoted so much to over the years of my life if they'd treat me like this and move on so easily?

19

Lost Souls—Buried Alive

Being in prison I witnessed first hand the depth of a human life as its own soul suffered dai y from being cut short to live out its full existence. Men with life prison sentences and in jails fighting severe prison time that have become unrecognized innocent martyrs in the justice system perils. Understand the weight of never being able to enjoy the simple luxuries of life again made abundantly clear. Men of their 20's and 30's years of age, in the prime of their strength, both in mind and body, rotting away their existence in jails and prisons, and oppressed still while free.

Nothing in all my experiences astonishes me so much as the continued neglect of these unfortunate souls by society. Every face has a history, every life a story, if we but take the trouble to read, acknowledge, and understand. The face is but an index of the heart, and even in the heart of the happiest the "Muffled drums are beating". My hope is that one day the outside world will be inspired to see them for their giftedness and abilities.

Jesus tell us that we will be hated by the world. We are constantly bombarded with negativity such as anger, fear, deception, and depression. Even the strongest in faith can start to get worn down. The constant hostile environment combined with solitude, cold air, and scanty food influences a dreadful state of helplessness and predator over prey mind state, even when presented with sympathetic actions. The constant predation inflicted upon them making them in turn so treacherous themselves that they can not believe in the sincerity of others.

In most cases the devotion of a loving family has died under these combined conditions of far off situated prisons built in small prairie farm lands miles away from their homelands. Lost souls having the feeling of being forgotten and kicked to the curb. This leads directly to a feeling of disconnection from society, from self, and a disenfranchisement. A constant emotional process of the betrayal, and the loss and feeling forgotten. All the makings for an intense rage to foster within.

Prisons succumb to become valleys of the living dead, harboring social stigmas seeking to dehumanize us; pariahs of society, forgotten men, women, and children.

In my own incarceration, I had to remain faithful instead of hopeful. Motivated instead of wishful thinking. At times I tried every spiritual means I knew to throw off the depression that descended on me and shrouded my head and shoulders. I read the Bible faithfully everyday—all day. The limited food supply was akin to severe fasting already. I did that with intense prayer and fasting. At such times the depression lifted for awhile, but inevitably it returned. Each time it did, my hopelessness grew deeper. My anxiety became disabling, and the continued solitude was madness in it purest nature.

No life form created by gods creation should be subjected to the evils of confinement such as NRC-Stateville Prison. 24 hours repeatedly locked in a cell, one phone call and one shower a week routine without windows, no exposure to sunlight or natural air; meal portions the size of lunchables snack trays. If one didn't die in his cell physically by the conditions endured, then surely his soul died, his spirit passed away, emotionally despondent to the naturalness of life that a human-being essence is endowed with, but now void of.

These constructed "Corrections" centers are spirit-breaking centers and as is titled but just the opposite of corrections. Parolees return to society as numbful, emotionally void persons, robbed and victimized to the extent that they have become victimized if not more than the persons they were convicted of committing crimes against according to the law. Justice is never served in this manner, it just creates the mechanisms for repeat offenders who feel a violation has been committed against them unfairly, and due course now manifested a revengeful spirit if met with repeated oppression instead of support and kindness; ingraining feelings of unworthiness, powerless in improving themselves and their conditions.

So why not become just as ruthless as they have been portrayed and treated as to be? Why not exact the state of vengefulness against a society of people who has forgotten them and enslaved them, and shun them?

With a tamed soul and broken spirit of a slave, how can one ever be free? Who truly benefits from this?

20

Money Pit–Incarceration Costs

A Billion-Dollar a year net revenue industry: The Prison System benefits at the costs of human lives misery. From the victims of crimes, the law-makers, lawyers, criminals charged, and jails and prisons that house them. On closer inspection, individually, who really benefits from prisoners incarceration other than the collect phone call corporations; the inflated commissary food order fulfillment companies; and prisoner apparel and linen, and prison construction companies?

These facilities get their operating costs payments from the state and federal government at a rate of per inmate housed. It's here further advantages is taken of by ridiculously expensive collect phone calls, video visitations, commissary, and private lawyers. These costs the individual incarcerated and his love ones dearly in weekly expenses. It becomes a bottomless pit of expensive transactions for the person lucky enough to have the money to make commissary orders; lucky to have someone answer your collect phone calls by constantly putting money on the phone charge account that could run up to as much as $12 for 15 minutes a local call in state with nearly $4 just for the first minute. A 15-minute phone call to family can cost more than $10.

Over half the people incarcerated were poor prior to being incarcerated, and their family income reduces dramatically while they are away, if not all together. Their families bear the burden of sending money for phone calls and commissary purchases.

Moreover, take in account the gas and transportation costs for your love ones to make the trike to visit a prisoner then be subjected to demeaning and dehumanizing body searches. Communications companies like Securus Technologies monopolize on prison system in a 360 degrees platform format to cover phone calls, email messaging services, video visitations, downloadable music marketplace with games on a media tablet.

Inmate commissary fulfillment companies like Keefe inflate regularly priced items outside the prison system by double or quadruple its regular in stores price. For instance, A Ramen Noodle priced at a local grocery store for .19 cents would be sold to an inmate for .62 cents or as much as a $1.25 in some facilities. The Bob Barker Corporation has made billions from selling cheaply constructed and fabricated inmate shoes, prison uniforms, sheets, blankets, inmate underwear, and towels to jails and prisons nationwide.

Prison construction companies build out prisons at double the rate new schools are funded for needed upgrades, teacher salaries, and supplies for students. Its a capitalize concept market that funnels money in the pockets of lobbyists and state lawmakers to create harsher laws to in effect have longer sentences for persons convicted of these crimes and make longer prison stays incarcerated to keep or to receive more state and federal funds from tax payer dollars.

The cost of prosecution in the Federal Bureau of Prisons is $103 daily, $3,121 monthly, and $37,448 annually. A ridiculous amount when you could've just given him a job instead. Inmate care at off site facilities receiving $4 million dollars a year in federal small jails, and at $60 a day per inmate housed in state jails and prisons.

This sinister system also lets attorneys capitalize off it in a false perception of grandeur in a court better described as a Shakespearean play, whereby the defendant is the only one ignorant and led astray about the grand scheme of things being played against him by the attorney, prosecutor, judge, and purposeful misleading coded laws. A system that capitalizes off a victims misfortune to rally up support from them for harsher sentencing laws against persons convicted of not only violent crimes, but also gun possession, drug possession, and crimes against properties. Unbeknownst to the mislead supporter of the monetary gain objective at play. It is ultimately the poor and middle-class taxpayer victim who will fit the bill for the prison construction, upkeep, and prison care of the very person who has committed an offense against them or their neighbors. A blind investment without any profitable returns.

Who is the bigger criminal? The one who made $200 off of drug sales on your block; or the robber who took $200 of your money at gunpoint; or perhaps the one who has and will take more than 50% of your hard earnings over your life time, totaling millions?

21

Return On Investment–
Tax Dollars

The ignorant public at large doesn't inquire as to where their tax payments are going. If they did, they'll discover a large majority isn't going to fund the construction of roads, build schools, or implement programs to aid the disenfranchised. It funds the prison system; to build more jails and prisons; payroll judges, prosecutors, corrections and police officers; house and feed inmates picked up on everything from heinous murders and rapists to petty theft and disorderly conduct.

Taxpayers spend their lifetime and half their earnings for supporting this system of cycled corruption and supporting laws that increase the continued negative effects on black and brown communities. Large sums of money are expended in maintaining public institutions that we call prisons, in which they are kept for short and long periods of time, and in which they submitted to lives of semi-idleness. Taxpayers dollars for feeding and housing inmates that sit around doing nothing that gives a notable return on investment.

Large numbers of warders and officers are maintained to look after them when in prison; large numbers of police are required to look after them when they are at liberty. Innocent people suffer through their depredations; honest and hard-working people, have to keep then when they are submitted to the comparatively comfortable life in prison and future generations bear the heavy burdens because of this, robbed of funding that could have went to their education, programs in assisting with sufficient public housing, food distributions, and healthcare.

Taxpayers need to count your money, and is it worth it to allow your hard-earned money to feed, clothe, and house a person arrested for selling drugs or theft to feed their hungry family? When instead they could be using that money to help feed their family and helping that individual back to his feet so they're able to do it on their own without resulting to criminal activity as a means to procure money.

No one benefits more from incarceration than the person who doesn't pay taxes and provides the services to the prison system, which are one of the same. Taxpaying citizens pay taxes that pays for the construction and upkeep of jails and prisons, which employs the security, building maintenance, food, healthcare, clothing, and housing. Taxpaying citizens pay for public defense attorneys, judge, police, prosecutors to arrest, try, and convict an inmate, who the taxpaying citizen family will additionally pay for; private defense attorneys, collect phone calls, commissary orders, missed meals, emotional turmoil, and cataclysmic lifestyle alterations because of the loss of a love one and the ensuing legal battle.

Society needs to take advantage of these 4 million incarcerated individuals, and instead of paying your taxes to feed, house, and clothe these people while they rot away in prisons and jails, then return to society with nothing; give them the opportunities they need like housing, education, employment, and transitional services that aren't binding to their freedom when they do still have the blessings of a adequate support system to aid in their transition from family, friends, and love ones. And thats not to say to turn a blind eye to violent repeat offenders for new crimes committed, but instead, individualize that persons sentence accordingly instead of setting a flat bar for everyone that doesn't deserve it.

Prisoner skills are wasted to prison sentences instead of re-distributed back to constructive development within the communities they come from, or servitude to victims altered because of the crimes committed against them. My pains are severity to witness the suffering on both sides in which men are taken away from their families, and young children robbed from the opportunity to grow up without their father in their lives, myself included.

On the other side of looking in, you may say don't do the crime if you can't do the time, but what greater crime is it not to assist your fellow man or neighbor when they stumble and fa l, to help rise back on their feet. Pay it forward. Demand your rightful return on investment, and to make right the wrongs he's committed against you.

How can you constructively repay your debt to society when its society that will ultimately in reality being the one paying your debts, literally, in taxes to feed inmates, house them, clothe them, on these unnecessary extended sentences. If it's a monetary repayment issue, then allow him to square away his debt. If he's hurt this man, in whatever way, at what point do we take in account his victims recommendation of what they deem an appropriate sentence?

People see's nothing to condemn in itself, forgetful that the sins they are committing may be greater in the sight of god than the sins which they are condemning in others. There are none so low, none so degraded as to be beneath consideration. To take the hand of the hardest criminal will not contaminate— vice is not contagious, but the support of constant oppression of a single class of people is genocidal massacre.

22

Generation Genocide–
Last Of A Dying Breed

It's as if nothing we do can change the current of our lives. The hand of fate is over all, leading us on, whether it be for good or for ill from the cradle to the grave, from birth to death, there is a power ruling our destinies. But without effort and change, human life cannot remain good. Those who profit by the existing order have established a system which punishes originality to opposition and starves imagination outside the normalcy programmed propaganda, from the moment of first going to school down to the time of death and burial.

Understanding casualty loss of potential warriors to prisons and grave yards, drug addicted zombies and homosexuality, traders and paid spies. These warriors make up generations of leaders, teachers, and beacons of hope to carry on their family's safety, protection and training of our youth to counter centuries of direful poverty combined with almost complete isolation from the economic progressive life of the world. The warriors left are embattled to strive threw racism, economic oppression, poverty stricken circumstances, and embedded violent traumas.

All in all it has not been able to take from them their look of race, or corrupt their brave, loyal, proud hearts. However rich and educated they might be, they are still uniformly kept trampled down in a degraded and irritating position, merely on account of their skin color. Black great heroes cut down for voicing their opposition to the injustices continually applied against them. All well-induced intimidation tactics to exert domineering force over to ensure you won't rise to greater pinnacles of society.

At a young age I could not help but thinking that such this would likely be my fate when I was older. Everywhere I looked was grimness: single moms working endless hours to provide; crackheads and dopefiends; gangbangers and dope dealers surviving. A eat or be eaten atmosphere. Inner cities are worlds in of themselves out to either harden or break your heart until you become insensible to pain and loss.

I didn't get raised in a household with sayings and someone guiding me along the way, I was just expected to know what to do and had to learn on my own and got punished for my mistakes and fuck ups. At some point I realized what my purpose of living was; the betterment for my children.

As for some parents, brought up to be slaves of custom, carry on the imbecile traditions that have been handed down to them from former generations, without stopping to consider whether they are rational or foolish. Culture and customs not of his own but celebrate figures not of native race.

A certain kind of self-respect or native pride is necessary to a good life; a man must not have a sense of utter inward defeat if he is to remain whole, but must feel the courage and the hope and the will to live by the best that is in him, whether outward or inward obstacles he may encounter.

Men and women now but children to a generation period of culture proud and steel clad inner resolve unmediated by tempting sensual enjoyments. Spiritually strong lines along the length of its communities out to protect and its own even at the costs of their own lives. It's a generation dying out leaving to surface its product of a few like minded individuals willing to sacrifice their lives for the greater good of its race, its family, and its seeds. But these seeds will be flourished in a burned soil over the scorch earth of designer drugs, advanced weapons, and negative influential propaganda set out to destroy them from their inception.

23

Born Losers—A Future Unfulfilled

To believe there isn't any hope for the youth is to say there isn't any hope for the future. A generation lost to roam the wilderness of the world without guidance is predetermined to be part of the collective losers of society, making up the common stock to substitute the generations lost before to the crack epidemics and mass incarcerations.

It is from the height of ones own self-reflected purity that they look with scorn upon some less fortunate mortal. But instead of turning away in disgust, examine closely the underlying outer crust of wickedness and sin, and you will be astonished at the amount of good you can find, even in the most depraved. It seems a crime for a child so young to have to endure so much.

Personally, I knew first-hand the lasting effects of stolen innocence. True products of their environments. Growing up in chaos robs children of ever having a real childhood and they will become men and women far sooner than other little boys and girls their age. Childhoods that are cruel to the point of being inhumane, and will carry the scars of their abuse into adulthood.

Understand first, it is hard for children born in slavery to grow up spiritually straight and emotionally healthy, because they are trodden on when they are little. Being constantly treated unjustly, they cannot learn to be just. Their parents have no power to protect them from evil influences. They cannot prevent their continually seeing cruel and indecent actions, and hearing profane and evil words, still the responsibility rests entirely onto the parent to educate your children, either morally or intellectually. Your influence exerted over the young souls entrusted to your care will be a rearing for eternity.

Children do not possess the perseverance and determination which often come to the rescue of original genius at a later period. However active their minds may be, they are also timid, and shrink back quickly under the influence of unsympathetic treatment.

Blacks with mental health short-comings can look forward to higher dropout rates in school, lower wages, higher rates of incarceration along with a propensity to abuse drugs and alcohol. Exposure to violence is a big part of black peoples' overall existence.

Children are particularly vulnerable. For example, children who see violence against their mothers experience the same psychological effects as if they were being physically abused. Children and teens in high poverty and high violence neighborhoods witness more than their fair share of stabbings, shootings, or sexual assaults. These are contributing factors to young people's lack of empathy, hyper-aggression and lack of trust of adults.

The fact remains even the most intelligent people find the utmost difficulty in attempting to shake off the prejudices inculcated during their early years of life. A fathers absence due to incarceration such as mine becomes a prevalence for my children to become prey to the evils of the world out to consume their naive minds and innocent bodies.

Standing fears that my daughters could become teenagers and pregnant; to grow up with "Daddy Issues" resulting in her being in a relationship with someone who will take advantage of her vulnerability in seeking a male influence and fatherly love from individuals who are not their father. Utter fear that they may succumb to pursue deprived issues with drugs and alcohol, sexual promiscuously outlets in a multitude of men for a man's attention.

I share the fear with millions of men and women that our sons, because they're growing up without our guidance and protection, may be enthralled into gang lifestyle of drugs, violence, and prison. I don't want him to die at the hands of the streets or a racist white cop. Kids need exemplary examples to live up to. Extreme responsibility is required to keep kids from thinking gangs and putting in work is cool.

The gang life of GD's, Latin Kings, Stones, Vice Lords, Bloods, and Crips is all fun when a young soul is surrounded by the feeling of being part of something until you're hit with a life sentence after putting in work or paralyzed and confined to a wheelchair after being shot multiple times, or worse killed or an innocent family member is killed for retaliation.

From young ages inner cities youth are consistently numbed greater and greater by the violent deaths and poverty conditions around them, and greater still by violent images and videos accessed online to the point of normalcy to have seen or known personally someone who has died violently; and emotional cruelty by the steady subjections to racism. The constant police harassment and suspicion of criminal activity puts a grim outlook perspective for little black boys.

Current times has made everything so expedient required that the youth rather rob and steal than hustle and work; women looking for a way out by any means necessary, rather it be stripping, prostitution, scamming, stealing, robbing, and willing to sacrifice their integrity and dignity just to portray a false perspective lifestyle they want to mirror as seen on social media.

Circumstances have turned households inside out, vindictively putting women against the very men they had children with and use the children as weapons against the fathers.

All these hateful actions rob the children of the love, attention, and affection they need to develop wholly.

It is the children in these deprivations who suffer entirely, and in turn society's future suffers. If they are not protected from risks in which they are too young to understand, and from attacks they don't have the developed wisdom to neither avoid nor resist, then they are teaching themselves how to live and survive in madness, and they become the very monsters who you wish against.

24

Birth Of A Monster—
Society's Creation

I was once told by a psychiatrist that my "Abnormal" reactions in most circumstances were actually "Normal". He went on to say abnormal behavior to abnormal circumstances is normal. Take for example a person brought up around violence, gangs, and drugs would naturally subject himself to the things of his environment, which would be not out of the normalcy that he has been surrounded by resulting in being a product of his environment.

Another perspective is a discovered cheating significant other. The reaction could produce a violent emotional or physical outbursts. This is where the law excuses crimes of passion to be used as a defense on psychoanalysis view, because under normal circumstances would produce normal behavior, but a abnormality such as of this emotionally shocking magnitude would of course give way to abnormal behavior in light of.

The same applicability has standing circumstances under "Drug Dealers Duress"; a term I coined to describe a persons decision to pursue sales in the drug market when they've been denied meaningful employment, housing, and to prevent homelessness, starvation, and subjection to the elements without proper clothing or money for transportation. This of course puts together the abnormal mental activity to attune to this abnormal survival tactics needed to weather his circumstances, which would be normal.

Under the normal circumstances of having a proper support system to aid him in his difficulties absent employment and other needs he wouldn't in affect choose to pursue drug sales or any other illegal activity.

What the vast public fails to realize is the growing resentment that festers inside the heart of a person locked up. While he sits his days away, often starving to the point of delirium, he remembers all the phone calls that go unanswered, letters not responded to, visitations neglected, and money to his trust fund account unacknowledged. The loneliness allows evil to enter, and a monster is created.

Payback and redemption consumes his thoughts now. The world will feel the pain and torment I've suffered in continuously for years. To be confined for making a way out of the suffering I was already subjected to by selling drugs, I felt an injustice was furthered committed against me. Punishing someone for actions that were pursued in survival efforts is an inhumane protocol, and prison just makes people more violent prone because of the hostile environment subjected to.

Most people don't understand the diminishment of social personality that comes from isolation. The compounded layers of resentment and hurt from being deserted by love ones. Now a "Eliminate Whatever Threat That Comes My Way" develops, whether it be real danger or just fictitious. And aggressive defensive behavior consequently surfaces whenever life and liberty are attacked. It is counter-intuitive to think that the labyrinth of social economic and political decisions that push black people into virtual and objective corners should not illicit a hostile response.

This was my reality. In a short time I was painfully reminded of the uncertainty of my condition after the cell doors closed and locked behind me. Placed into a position to either relent to blind submission or revolt against the oppression subjected to. I had had enough of just surviving instead of thriving. In my eyes, society as a whole has unconsciously agreed to turn its back on me and outcast me to the level of worthless and forgotten. This revelation also motivated and inspired me with vengeful hope, and I seized every opportunity to improve myself.

Given the opportunity to return, most releasees are hopeful but hopeless, defeatedly fearful but methodical in further future actions. Heart-harden intensely and emotionally void but utterly vulnerable to the reception of love, care, and support. So it is in this moment what he is given that he will react to.

If hostility and rejection supplied; then it will be met with savagery and cruelty, a parasite to society. If its love and support; then its loyalty and redemption, a rewarding return on investment.

How much would have been lost to myself and the world if I had remained a slave in prison, not allowed to profit by my own industry, and forbidden to improve my mind by learning to read, write, and apply constructively?

The abandonment by a woman or love interest intensifies the monster complex while incarcerated. The ordinary conventional thinking man placed in these circumstances would either throw a woman over, or marry her still afterwards reconnecting against his convictions. Having gone through such intense suffering by leaving that his or her character is probably deepened thereby and his or her capacity for love and faithfulness increased.

It is another truism that suffering is necessary to bring out the best qualities in men and women. But under these sufferings could also manifest the worse evils never intended to surface in man, therefore it is also necessary to have courage, for strength without self-confidence is useless.

It is sufficient enough to mention here just as children, natural enough, when you have preached at and punished a boy until he is a moral cripple, you are as much hampered by him as by a physical cripple; and as you do not intend to have him on your hands all your life. But the boys bewilderment by your inconsistency of wishes and demands will conclude that there is no use in trying to please you, and falls into an attitude of sulky resentment; emotions don't even come close to the rage and frustration of the young black men who've been criminalized and who must endure incessant police harassment and abuse on a daily basis without equal protection under the law. So why not become the problematic pursuer you continuously make him out to be?

25

Civil Death–
Return To Society

Post-incarceration syndrome created within self after years of being locked up makes it hard to quickly adapt to regular civilian life. Returning to society showcases the emotional mixture most parolees are unconscious of or afraid to being vulnerable to or heart-harden by the circumstances of serving time.

Dealing with people who only fucked with you because it was beneficial to them stays in the back of their minds, but usually so thankful to get their freedom at last, that there are no room in their hearts for bad feelings. But a far different state of mind, and body exists when they are released from authority, for with liberty the old instinct or passion comes into fierce existence, and instantly demands gratification.

While the released person has on the one hand gained considerably in health of mind and body, the sleeping passion too has gained in strength during the time it has hibernated. For they are helpless before the stress of temptation. It could take but the slightest breeze to revert to their old life. Defendants now at this stage become victims of the system.

Courts have sucked out household income that leads up to incarceration for failure to pay, loss of jobs and maybe even loss of housing that results in homelessness. After serving sentences they are still subjected to further civil penalties with barriers preventing access to housing, job training, and treatment they need to get on with their lives.

Like many parolees, my biggest fears was my reality; I was a 36 year old convicted felon having to start all over from scratch. It was absolutely quintessential that I had several methods and avenues to level up of just having the basics: A place of my own; a car; a job; clothing and a cellphone. I didn't have the blessings of support anymore. This would have to be all done on my own; with the determining factors of being homeless, broke, and defeated.

The return back requires to be well-equipped with the basics of shelter, clothing, transportation, and income stream. It's a strenuous recovery process, not only financially, but emotionally as well. Fighting through persistent, crippling bouts of depression; sincerely seeking legal success for my life, but was so oppressed by the continuing sense that I could never expect to succeed. The civil ramifications in again obtaining employment, housing, and family ties, add to the effect of new emotional and mental problems because being an ex-felon. It's a handicap label, as the public respect level for you decreases once knowledge of a criminal record is discovered or revealed.

In relationships, women disrespect by demeaning and belittlement as if your worth as a human-being has been lowered. So to talk down on him is validated in their eyes. Employers deny job applications summarily at all stages of various industries even when adequately skilled. Dismissive that We have to work. If we stop we starve.

There isn't even an honest place for ex-felons in the military. They are not good enough to be shot at! They are not good enough to shoot at others. The American government feels you're not good enough to be a recipient of a bullet. It is at this point ex-felons will begin to lose their fear of prison and grosser crime will follow. Men too weary from the heart-breaking and ceaseless search after employment, endless toil, and semi-starvation. Clear faith and well-grounded hope can only take you so far. There's a void in the atmosphere in which such things are possible for positive development to flourish.

My existence couldn't shake the growing anxieties of the challenges ahead of me. Uncertain of where I would live again, how would I make money to feed, clothe, and or even begin in repairing relationships lost to my incarceration. It is millions more faced with these same life alternating questions. Unsure of how to address, and incapacitated at nearly every opportunity to remedy. Even my utter ignorance activated the same mechanisms as hairbreadth escape from death tore my eyes open from the swathings of conventional opinion with which I had been blinded.

Instead of regarding myself as a deeply wronged man, I now realized that I had behaved inconsiderably horrible to the unfortunate woman, who had left me because of my incarceration. But now refused to be a man of such narrow views, and given to such harsh judgement. I now ask the public at large to do the same when considering men who have suffered well-merited terms of imprisonment. The community ought to receive them back with open arms.

By the term of imprisonment suffered, the law has been satisfied; and the law now holding them guiltless, nothing else ought to be considered. It has disastrous effects. If there is one virtue that is absolutely necessary to be discharged prisoners success, it is the virtue of self-reliance. Without it he is nothing. Without self-reliance he is a certain failure. Anything that tends to lessen self-reliance in discharged prisoners has been parole terms. Compelling a person to retain self-reliance but still hindered by electronic monitoring, mandatory curfew hours, restrictions on where they can live and go is an oxymoron of rules, like saying your free but not free.

The sight of a defeated and broken ex-prisoner touches me, and my heart goes out to him. Neither sympathy nor help will I deny him. A man that has committed some crime, and has then taken his gruel in both senses, who faces the world, and by pluck, perseverance, and rectitude regains his footing in life, is to me a hero; for I can appreciate his difficulties, and appreciate, too, his moral worth.

When a discharged prisoner possesses health, skill, and self-reliance, he has a hard battle to fight, one that will call forth either the best or the worst that is in him. The notable difficulties outside a prisons wall are so great that they cannot face them alone. But the saddest part of it is that they don't have to face them alone, and it must be confessed that they have not the slightest idea how to do so. We must look at things as they are.

Here are hundreds of thousands of young men who have no settled places of abode, no technical skills, no great physical strength, no supreme capabilities, and no desire for continuous hard labor with low wages. No one can provide them with employment. There is no place for them in industrial life, they are content to spend their lives in cheap lodging-houses or in prison. They beg or they steal when at liberty. Occasionally they do a little work, when it comes available. They gradually sulk in idleness and crime; they become habituated to prison, and finally they become hopeless criminals. It's a concrete ball and steel linked chain fastened around the ankle that all ex-felons will carry with them forever.

26

Ball And Chains—
My Own Oppressions

All my life I had been under oppression, even at the heights of the dope game when the money was plentiful. I continued taking chances. Why would a man with so much to lose be so careless? Because I had always taken chances and never been caught. Because it was a way of life, and even after being caught and taking a significant loss, I would soon return to my old ways. I figured the thrill of chasing paper and making something outta nothing over-shadowed the risks. It was at these times more personal adversities occurred with intense frequency, ultimately landing me in prison.

After serving prison time it felt strange to be free. I had accomplished more in jail in a four years bid than most people I knew free, and I made more money and educated myself well in having a plan going forward free. But I discovered quickly that freedom was normal and that oppression was abnormal.

Deep down I knew though I was out of prison, I was far from being free. Now having to contend with a term of electric monitoring, restrictions on work proximity's, and curfew orders on top of reconnecting with my children relationships, being broke, and emotionally tax'd being around the very Ex who broken my spirit.

Furthermore challenges in getting employment without reliable transportation; felony convictions without recent work field experience. I still pressed on, and was able to secure a car on the strength of my good credit I had worked on repairing while locked up and an apartment through a friend, and shortly got a call back for a job as a warehouse associate through a temporary work agency.

The pay was low and the work was back breaking, but it was an honest pay that I needed for the time being until I could secure a better job. But for months I was repeatedly hired by fortune 300 and 500 companies after interviewing and reviewing my skills and experience, but then turned around to have the offer of employment rescinded after discovering my criminal convictions for drugs. Yet in still, informed me that I was a qualified candidate but hindered because of the drug conviction and recent date of conviction. Telling me had I took the guilty plea immediately after being arrested instead of trying to defend against the charges for three years, I'd be eligible for hiring.

These many hiring managers for major corporations and industry leaders went on to tell me if it was a conviction other than for drugs, like a gun, a murder, or even sexual abuse, my chances for being hired would be better. It was disheartening to remember the lengthy torture I had just endured still haunting me.

I was brutally beaten by 3 Chicago police officers, then arrested on bogus trumped up criminal charges to cover their dirty deeds. After defending my case in County Jail after 3 years, I took the plea because the constant delays were draining and my children cried and begged routinely for my return to them. I was angry to be categorized with a whole of criminals, but the real criminals had been these same Chicago police officers that arrested me.

It wasn't my first time coming across their type; I was kidnapped and robbed, and had false charges placed against me by federal indicted Chicago police officers from the same precinct that the case inception extends from. It was an on-going retaliatory police harassment over a decade after I filed a federal civil lawsuit against the officers involved in that incident.

The bills and expenses I would began to accrue made no sense to continue to work at the warehouse with limited work and pay. My fresh parole status prevented me to take on good job opportunities and to get away from the influence of returning back to the streets. Parole and probation are just trap doors to keep offenders in the system. It helps no one. Benefits no one except the wealthy when they're recommitted to prison for violating the terms of parole or probation.

Acquiring employment wasn't the only uphill battle, it was also being discriminated against; trying to get approved for lease agreement by landlords was another after my apartment building caught fire leaving me homeless. Living out a hotel for months, hustling work again took the forefront for me to utilize to get back on my feet, unfortunately after finally doing so, I was arrested on a federal indictment for drug distribution 13 months after paroling from state prison.

I don't know which one made me angrier: being set up by a regular customer to assist his drug sale to an undercover cop that now held me on new charges; or the fact that the circumstances I was placed in made dealing drugs an almost unavoidable option to prevent starvation and homelessness.

The first couple of federal court dates I zoned out as the district attorney told the judge about my criminal history, the new charges against me, and how I was a danger to the community if released on bail. I smirked on the inside as I thought whose community was the white prosecutor referring to, because the sudden temptations to commit crimes in order to get away from the community I was raised in is caused by the stress of poverty, something the sea of white faces in the court room only know of by watching it on TV or reading about. I wanted to yell out and object to the prosecutors negative summarization perspective he intended to paint for the judge of my crime, character, and criminal history, because the scared shitless assigned attorney I had to represent me surely wasn't.

I resented deeply what all he had neglected to point out that I was not viewed on the undercover video recording doing like receiving cash in hand, or wasn't the main target of the Chicago Police investigation. The main target was released shortly after being in custody. I would however remain for a year and a half as of this writing.

I'd probably never get the opportunity to tell the court what the undercover video does show is the immense stress I was under on my facial expression, or that it shows the bundle of lettered bills in my passenger seat; the datebook folder in my lap containing a commercial drivers license study guide book; and that I was studying while I slept most nights in my car.

Additionally, what the prosecutor neglected to mention to the judge was that just as many times I've been arrested, over a dozen of them resulted in federal civil suits against Chicago police officers for false arrests, harassment, and retaliation for filing complaints and civil lawsuits for the on-going assaults, harassment, destruction of property, death threats, being kidnapped and robbed by officers from this same precinct and unit of police officers that was federal indicted for heinous crimes against Chicago residents—me included.

My defense attorney should have interjected to mention my own struggles and hardships in acquiring housing and employment because of my criminal record, mainly the one for which I paroled; an conviction obtained by near coercion means; or told the I was a writer and author, an inventor, and about my plans and ambitions to create non-profit organizations to help returning to society prisoners with immediate housing, employment, and transportation. He could've mentioned the volunteer work and charity Christmas gifts of a $1,000 in wrapped and donated toys to the red cross while I still lived out a hotel for five months after my apartment building caught fire and I loss everything. But it all would have landed on deaf ears. The kind that they could exact their negative judgements and preconceived notions upon.

They wouldn't care to understand a criminal case encompasses an individuals entire family too; that I'm a person too, and I have a family as well. I celebrate birthdays, holidays with my family just as all of you. I also dress and prepare the day for my children every morning, pick them up from school and help them with their homework afterwards. Children utterly heartbroken because I've missed there birthdays and holidays over the years. That I've suffered plenty, and the absence has been severe punishment in of itself.

Taunted with the memories of being up all night decorating the Christmas tree with my daughter, and my sons face when he seen it finished. It was a bleak reminder, that I would still be judged different than them rather I showed up in a fine tailored suit and tie respectfully or in the black and white stripped jail jumpsuit.

Early in the re-incarceration I knew first hand the relationships I had built while free wouldn't last long under the circumstances. My last experience was a valuable teacher. It was no good in expecting a young girlfriend to behave like ones mother. It took three years of grief before the thought arisen that she had scarcely time to realize what youth meant and begin to enjoy it before her girlhood was stifled under the responsibilities of a committed relationship and maternity.

A decade earlier, I had met her at the age of 19, beyond me she had seen nothing of men, just boys, or the world even with the five years age difference between us. At twenty-six, my son mother begin to realize that she had been cheated out of a very precious part of life and an invaluable experience when I went away.

A dangerous spirit of curiosity entered her heart, and still more dangerous longing for adventure and excitement that I wasn't there to supply. By the age of thirty, she had engineered over more than several affairs. The abandoning grief so serious for me, impacting me to remove all understanding, tenderness, care, and love from my existence in order to make it through my remaining prison term. If only she would had the single woman in her 20's excitement, gaiety, and glamour first, then we met.

Normally, my features were well formed, and large dark eyes were bright and expressive. A manly air, motions easy and dignified, and altogether I loved life passionately for its own sake before my incarceration. I lead a vivid life that reflected an intellectual face, full of fiery energy and calm resource. I've always had the aura of a thinker and been a fighter in one. Looked like a being that would never consent to wear a chair and shackles. Jail had rendered me pale and thin from hardships and the long confinement. It was then I got to a point that I realized I had to focus so ely on myself in order to rebuild and become a better self. Deciding not to complain about how I was tired of living and enduring, and how life has never been all good, just surviving. I had refuse to cower behind stress and worry any further that wasn't practical. Nor was it practical in dating women with similar undiagnosed mental disorders of bi-polar depression (2nd Baby-Mother), cutter and promiscuous (Ex-Girlfriend), in an effort to secure comfort and security from abandonment problems (3rd Baby-Mother).

I've considered others needs over that of my own while they still held attachments to Ex's, ir tattoos, kids, material items, and emotional baggage. Fixing up there homes and cars when my own shit wasn't prepared in a greater fashion. Working through street beefs, being kidnapped and robbed at gunpoint four months after being released from prison; robbed at gunpoint a week later; and still rummaging to put my life back together. needed time to get my own priorities in order first. How could I fill the next persons cup if mines was empty?

Losing all fear restraints was liberating but I also was numb to things most people would mentally and emotionally crumble under. I was comfortable in the chaos, numb to the pains that various devastating trials and tribulations incubated, became just as unforgiving, self-centered, and thoughtless as the people who treated me with the same fashions. The caged ruthlessness of an attacked apex animal would now become part of my ingrained existence. Wounds of which ran deeper than surface level.

27

Whip Wounds & Scars—
PTSD & Emotional Turmoil

Having the sense of inferiority so early impressed on the minds of a single race, assassinates any hopes to rise to greater power and character. Emotional scars become surface level even decades after initial inceptions of racial profiling, violent and excessive force arrests or stop and frisked. Prison terms that forever change a persons otherwise normal mental make up into one of an emotionally voided or unavailable and predatory processed in order to survive by any means necessary.

PTSD is woven into the very fabric of every black persons DNA. Especially those ravaged by poverty and violence. yet, when we see or experience the behaviors of those affected, our initial tendency is to criminalize the behavior. It is post traumatic slave syndrome. A on-going trauma that envelops the daily lives of people of African descent in this country. Cellular level traumas passed through generations of slave descendants.

Who can bear the thoughts of his relatives being torn from him by a savage enemy; carried to distant regions of the habitable globe, never more to return. Fathers and mothers sold away from children. Children torn from them without being allowed to bid them goodbye. Tortured slaves, cruelly whipped and branded with hot iron, hunted and torn by bloodhounds, and even burned alive, merely for trying to get their freedom.

There had been so much of the separation of families in slavery; had gone through so much suffering and terror, that it is remembered with bitterness of heart, how growing up without a father one found his way through the life of darkness without the light of a leader, the most important one, of the household.

Coming of age, my mind had become bewildered concerning the past. A constitution that never recovered from the shock it had received in early childhood of poverty, violent incidents, and loneliness. Admittedly, I loved to a madness, and lost love to a ghost of that dead passion forever. Now just a poisonous presence that kills the joy when in reminiscence, for the memory is a potent poison.

Understanding the human heart is a strange compound made up love and hate, of joy and sorrow, hope and despair. Who is able to understand the sorrows, struggles, and temptations of others without reflecting it upon themselves first? And who is competent to take upon himself the task of judging? How can we believe in the goodness and loving kindness of god, when we see nothing but coldness and selfishness in our fellow creatures? Would it not be well to teach and train the human mind to the belief that any act committed which is injurious to ourselves or our fellow creatures is wrong, because the act in itself is wrong and not because we are to be punished in the future? Leave out the doctrine of reward and punishment, teach and train the mind to something higher and holier than mere personal gratification, and consideration for the stumbles of others.

Limited empathy, being one of the bad customs which grows out of slavery: slavery was producing its natural fruits of tyranny and hatred, cruelty and despair; and there are not many people who are conscientious about being kind in their relations with human beings. Their oppressors have made them afraid to use their speech to complain of their wrongs. Therefore, those who have been slavishly oppressed know how to sympathize with others of similar oppressions.

The dispositions of men and women, bad-tempered and stubborn, it is owing to their having been badly treated when they were young. Such treatment produces an unwillingness to oblige the tormentor.

To be compelled to constantly bear the burden of large loads of responsibilities and expectations too heavy for their strength, makes them angry and discouraged; and at last, in despair of getting any help for their wrongs, they stand stock still in their anger, discouragement, and depression. Apparently coming to the conclusion that it is better to be killed at once than to die daily.

The great problem of slavery for those whose aim is to maintain it is the problem of reconciling the efficiency of the slave with the hopelessness that keeps him in servitude. Self-preservation forces him to break the spirit that revolts against him, and to inculcate submission, even to obscene assault, as a duty. The poor however never escape from servitude, their docility is preserved by their slavery. And so all become the prey of the greedy, the selfish, the domineering, the unscrupulous, the predatory.

If here and there an individual refuses to be docile, ten docile persons will beat him or lock him up or shoot him at the bidding of his oppressors and their own. Who can you trust then? It is a loathsome feeling of constant inferiority that reigns supreme like a dark cloud forever following over the black race in America. It is a wrong still not righten; one of which equals to making us believe we are not worth it to be acknowledged as done so. If I am inferior, then who is superior? If I am less than who is great? If I am soiled, dirty, wicked, evil, and sullen—per the Merrian-Webster dictionary, then who is clean, pure, good, and innocent?

One of the most insidious things about white supremacy is it has the power to make you doubt yourself: did I get looked over a promotion or not be hired because my skin color? Did my credit application or service was poor because of my race? Are there any breaks of overt oppression living in a society that has been embedded with racism since it's beginning?

Just being black is an obstacle in of itself. A scolded impression burned into the mind and heart of every black person that has to contend with it. Now generations of pain is manifesting itself in front of the world. Young black men angry but don't know why really. Life stages that will formulate unexplainable anger within self unclear of its deep settled inception.

28

The Hurt Keeps Hurting–
Cycle Of Victimization

A many can be wronged from one wronged. It's as epidemic and contagious as fear. Geneticists believe that through our cells, information has been handed down from our ancestors over generations and centuries over the millennia, which explains our constant development to become smarter and more advanced. So can emotional pains be transitioned down as well? Bloodlines of traumas, hurt, and stress be recorded and contained in the DNA at the cellular level too? Is it then any wonder why blacks of inner cities sin cruelty against one another because they were cruelly sinned against?

Millions of blacks are inherently mourning for ancestors, relatives, love ones lost to slavery, and left to watch their families for centuries tortured, beaten, women and daughters raped, and sons lynched.

Descendants for 100 more years subjected to poverty, discrimination and oppression. Before you now is a raging generation, tired of the ill-treatments and judgements by others just because the color of their skin. Tired of encountering only hostile suspicion, aggression, and mistreatment. Tired of being the catalyst for crime statistics, brutal murders, victims of police brutalities, burned alive and shot dead in churches, hung from trees, shot dead in the open streets, left to die in prison cells, and tortured by witnessing the lives lost around them to crack, heroin and PCP.

You grow desensitized to the violence against you. Surmounting pains from living in urban war zones where children are shot dead by stray bullets and prey'd upon by predators operating in immunity to consequence. Being systemically generally neglected and abused because they themselves were accustomed to hard treatment. The pains makes us numb and therefore incorruptible by the evils of the world, or worse yet turn up to a sever degree than what we've been subjected to. Now at the stage of refusing to be bullied further into submissiveness. The victim becomes the victimizer.

What you have before you is a raging bull generation that's festered emotionally, spiritually, and mentally on the killings of our mothers, grandmothers, fathers and grandfathers that you continue to try and subjugate us to racial injustices.

Hell yes we're mad. We are angry as hell. We've got every right to be. The pent up manifesting anger and frustration is exploded outward if given the opportunity or contained further inward until implosion of self-destruction. Self-medicating with drugs and alcohol.

New opioids of designer drugs; Perks, Lean, Ecstasy, and Molly to suppress the pass traumas suffered. Addictions go further with cigarettes.

There is nothing so exhausting as uncontrolled emotion. Such courage to demonstrate does not wait for great occasion for exhibiting itself; it is revealed in the midst of the humdrum routine of daily life—a routine that is especially trying to those who have Benn looking forward to some great, perhaps dramatic service to release harbored expressions. Unfortunately most of the time they express negatively upon those closest such as a lover in demeaning belittlement of disrespect; violence against a child. Violence against neighbor.

Children witness these accounts as a valid way to release negative expressions in the forms of bully's, drug users, and crimes against people in the public. Being once someone's punching bag of bullying and brutal assaults or neglect, that resent is projected outward or inward as a form of self-unworthiness. This dissatisfaction must be gratified. In most cases it begins with trouble ascertaining or standing up for themselves; in another, individuals victimized when they were younger and prone to vulnerability may feel like; now that I'm in a position of power, I can exact that power over someone else who is utterly defenseless, powerless, and scared.

Understanding: Hurt People Hurt People. But as such also produces empathy. Having had my own growth stunted, from being trodden upon when I was little, will doubtless make you more careful not to tread upon children. Racism in America already has an essential long-standing abusive relationship. A collective fear and anxiety projected outward from both races Blacks fear whites in authoritative positions that can effect their life, liberty, and livelihood; whereas whites would fear blacks out of perpetuated stereotyped myths that they'll rob, rape, and murder them. These conceived perceptions are confronted violently when they meet, causing sure destructive behavior from both races.

Myself having plenty experience of revolting incidents in police encounters via aggressive white officers out to prove their power of dominance and racial prejudices or fear and jealously of a common black man; judges who has made it clear in their disdain for "My Kind"; everyday white citizens who turn their nose up to me because I can afford a place in their neighborhood or frequent the restaurants and shops they do. It's a fatal impression upon the minds of both races, rather they know it or not.

29

Conscious For The Unconscious– Understanding The Destructive Impact

At the young age of eight, I remember my first encounter with being called a nigger. It was after spending the day shopping with my mother at the Ridgeland mall. As we waited for the Pace bus, a black mustang pull alongside us with two young white men inside, and called us niggers as they pulled away in traffic. The racist insult made me feel inferior and out of place at a time I didn't know the depth of what I was feeling. Here it was we were just innocently waiting on the bus to come and was subjected to hateful insults.

Overtime I cringed with mounting resentment every time I seen a White man in person. Its also one of the reasons I was never good at advancing in math through my grammar school years because my math teacher was a White man. It was white men I witnessed growing up patrolling my neighborhood and harassing people of my skin color. It was white men I seen on TV beating, hanging, and setting ablaze men of my race.

In my teens, it was white men who violated my innocent perspective of friendliness to protect me. But instead they put handcuffs on me; called me nigger freely; beat me bloody; violated my body in dehumanizing searches, and ignored my rights as a human being. Every Blackman has a story to tell of an encounter with a white person and was subjected to racism and racist behavior.

As it stands, black communities have been classified for decades as "High Crime Areas". Cities of just one-third black populations are titled most dangerous part of the city, have the highest sexually transmitted diseases rates in U.S.; be the most racially segregated and racial mortgage rate disparities. Blacks unemployment rates exceed 3 times that of whites and black motorists are 100 times more likely to be stopped by police than whites.

Acknowledging it has been the evils of the White man who set the precedence of slavery in America through to oppression and poverty on a collective of people who only wanted the same as every other human being in the world: To live life peacefully; Have liberty; and the freedom to pursue happiness without oppression.

It amazes me of the considerable objective judgement looked upon of someone in my conditions. This is how you made me! My current circumstances are the result of the oppressive systems you've instilled. Where's there no education, but poverty, there will be violence and crime. You have allowed the criminal justice system to devastate family lives, and fail the people it imprisons and society pays for it in more ways than one by way of multitudes of families to be broken apart. These children grow into teenagers and adults disconnected to proper guidance, security, and education. Bound to repeat the same cycles of struggles and oppression their parents faced.

The best thing you can give children is a loving family— Together, if not, society and the public at large ultimately pays for this injustice in the form of criminals, disenfranchised communities, violent and misguided uncontained youth given easily to drugs, gangs, and preying upon the rest of well-off society to the point of victimizing them. The well-off part of society pays further in taxes, predatory devastating enacted criminal coded law statues that impact poor community residents worse.

We must hold ourselves up as a warning and not as an example to our children and society at large. To banish a parent away from their children is to allege that children are better with a parent continually away from home and to give up the whole popular sentimental theory of the family.

Even while I now write this book incarcerated, it is my 13 year old daughter and 8 year old son I have to explain my mistakes to, and that resulted in my absence. Imagine trying to raise children over the phone. When you sentence one person, you also sentence his entire family. It's the void they are also punished with because of his or her absence. It's the source of income they would now have to do without. The source of guidance, love, comfort, protection, and refuge they will now have to do without. Poss bly now ushering in a cycle of hurt, abandonment, and resentment.

My heart pains increasingly at the scenery of the destruction amongst my people. This may only be of a minority of given sympathizers to this notion. The experienced empathizer knows people so thoroughly, they will expect nothing more of you than you can give them, and will appreciate your virtues to the utmost and make the best of your vices. But as such any person who takes time to think on the subject can not fail to see that human misery is increasing. With all the boasted advantages of civilization, it has failed to bring happiness into the lives of the people. The more enlightened people become the more they will recognize the fact that knowledge does not bring happiness. Scientific discoveries do not tend to lighten the load of human misery. People are asking themselves daily; "Is life worth living", and most persons answer in the negative. The poor answer is a living example of everyday life.

By deepening our understanding of the roots of our psychological and mental trauma, we can stop blaming the victims and we can fully understand why black people hate themselves and each other. Our struggle for political and economic empowerment will be more holistic when we break the mental shackles from our minds and souls. We can turn our attention to the system of capitalism and white supremacy that keeps the wheels of trauma greased.

Efforts to change these dynamics must go first to dismantling the machine that produces misery among society. Being black in America already has its daily burdens. Driving while black. Walking while black. Jogging while black. Shopping while black. Biking while black. Watching television in your own home while black. Partying while black. Working while black. Talking while black. Praying while black. And the list goes on and on.

Black people have been killed by white people while doing all of the above. Over time, the racial oppression, the economic injustices, the police terror and the contemptuous attitudes gets normalized. Then one day the simmering cauldron of racism, economic exploitation and police violence bubbles over. The plains of enemies before you becomes clear as the haze evaporates, and you're able to prepare properly for battle. Eyes open, weapons ready, feet planted firmly into the soil.

To be aware is to be alive enough to recognize what you're up against.

30

War Machine—Recognizing The Battlefield

Only fools and romantic novices imagine that freedoms is a mere matter of the readiness of the individual to snap his fingers at convention. If men were born free, then by its proper bearing all men wouldn't long for freedom. it is on the contrary, they are enslaved by a capitalist system whose unmistakably vile results is understood by those who profit by it in money as by those who are starved and degraded by it. And yet the machine works so detestably at present against society.

The conscience of mankind has become drugged and lethargic, our minds are fixed upon sensual pleasures, and our conduct regulated by a blind struggle for the maximum of luxurious enjoyment. It is this utter distraction most people don't recognize the war going on. A everlasting fight for freedom.

It is by reason and investigation the we are permitted to partially understand the strange mysteries of a wonderful world. But as a poor person you are crippled from experiencing this. Purposely held in disadvantage for the advantage of the wealthy. If you are among the few who try and make a way out of poverty by illegal means, you could end up being part of the collective stock that make up a dollar count on a spread-sheet in the form of a human individual.

Lobbyists keep pressuring law makers for tougher laws on top of laws that are already harsh in order to disarm every poor and middle-class individual and make long-term permanent incarcerated residents for profit. The prisons and broken homes are all ways that are used to make the Blackman what he is not.

The Blackman is one of the most splendid creatures on the face of the earth. He is the ultimate prize, but keeps oppressors feeling less threaten while he's down trodden and behind bars.

In noticing that black and brown impoverished communities are immensely laced with alcohol stores, illegal drug markets, and guns that originate from states far from where their put to use. Is it any wonder they reflect war zones?

Whole communities uprooted and demolished to make the use of highway construction for the purpose of white development is not isolated to any just one city. Black neighborhoods are especially vulnerable because property values are low and could easily be acquired for little or nothing or through eminent domain. Like interstate 10 plowing through the thriving black business districts in New Orleans. Or St. Paul's Rondo Avenue, the heart of the city's largest black neighborhood where construction of I-94 shattered the tight knit and vibrant community displacing thousands of African Americans who had lived there for generations.

Public housing project structures in Chicago demolished that now sit as empty lots still and residents displaced throughout the Chicagoland.

Moreover, insidious city planners designed efforts to de-stabilize the African American communities back since in the mid-1970's, and is in full effect many decades later. The purposeful infliction of physical, emotional, psychological, cultural and economical and political injuries of the racist plan to discourage investment in the black areas, diminish city services and housing codes would be selectively enforced in order to add housing and land tracts to the city's land banks. The closings of hospitals and neighborhood schools have been early targets as the plan inferred that destroying major institutions in neighborhoods would have a domino effect and hasten its demise.

To not proactively combat racism and white supremacy acds to the problem. Because the general public believes what the news reports to them, we must challenge the racist imagery on the local news, and by teaching our children their self-worth, by ending racial profiling, by eliminating laws that specifically target blacks (such as drug laws), and by educating ourselves on how internalized racism affects us all.

Negative perceptions about blacks are at its created inception by white owned news and media, movies and newspaper; a constant propaganda that instills into the minds of people around the world that blacks are bad, dumb, and criminals.

The press has too long basked in a white world looking out of it with a white perspective, along with a president of the United States that publicly categorizes brown people as thieves, rapists, drug lords, and the worst kind of criminals on the face of the earth. This same public puppet is the kind of distraction constantly pushed forward on television, radio, and social media as a method to keep us distracted from the real issues keeping us oppressed.

It bothers me to a severe degree to constantly see black men portrayed on TV, news and media as sissy's; dressed in feminine attire; in women's make up, wearing purses and dresses; made to give young black men the impression that this is what they should ascribe to by its utter normalcy. No strong Blackman is demonstrated on white-owned media outlets. As such so we are not to be respected as real men. In the same outlets, gay white men dressed in the same garb are rarely shown to the same degree as black men.

Raising above our circumstances requires more than all smoke and mirrors presented in Civil Rights, we need more. Every culture has its own specific rights, muslim rights, latino rights, but still no Black rights. The earnest desire to improve our circumstances ought to be gratified against the vast machine-like organizations, governed from above by men who know and care little for the lives of those whom they control within an economic slavery, killing any opportunity for individuality and freedom of mind, and forcing men more and more to conform to a uniform pattern of being raised in poverty to short terms in a miseducation system and ultimately profited off on a criminal injustice system.

Those lucky enough not to be induced into this pattern are akin to farm animals braising near to the slaughter house boosting that they are above the subjection their brethren has succumb to.

31

Braising Cattle– Fictitious Freedom

When you realize how easy it is for your freedom to be taken away from you and to lose all you have worked hard to build and maintain; you notice you really never had true freedom in the first place. It's been a false sense of security provided by a constant simulation of social media, television programming, oppressive paycheck to paycheck work week hours, and schooling for degrees just to become another employee in society.

Drugs and alcohol add to this comatose state of unacknowledgement to break away from the programmed zombie mode. A constant stream of stimulus is provided to reach a presented goal, similar to a horse with a carrot outreached in front of it by the rider to make the horse go the distance at the horse riders bidding. Are there any who grasp the prize for which they have struggled?

Compounded by layers upon layers of required education stages to be recognized by so-called elite scholars and academia, if there are a few who succeed in reaching to the height to which they aspire, they find happiness is just as much beyond their reach as when they first started in their career. It is bitter mockery to say that the man who struggles for daily bread is happy. He may do his work uncomplainingly, but he cannot be happy.

If the real gone struggle while the fakes get all the glory, then there must be another form of snobbery which is not so easily recognized, and requires a good judge of human nature to detect. It is with grim reality that we are reminded our freedom and relaxing comfort comes at a price seemingly subtle but effective in keeping entirely free from monitoring inclusion. When you are snatched from your native land, taken away from all that is familiar to you, then forced to work for someone, any work relationship is doomed from the start.

You are not free if held slave to, such as the American healthcare system in only treating health aliments instead of curing them. It is a devious system from the outset to make you sick with cancer causing pollution, airborne containments, and dangerous mandated vaccines in children to set the stage for a later treatment client. Natural plant medicines have been around since time inmemorable to treat every human and animal disease on the surface of the earth. The billion-dollar pharmaceutical companies know this and has made it its mission to eliminate any known practitioners utilizing natural methods to cure persons. Aboriginal medicine men have made use of natural medicines for centuries but limited the teaches because of the white mans intrusion and thievery in America. Civilization at large suffers because of this.

America over the last decade has increased its surveillance of its citizens to have greater tracking and intelligence of all by systematically tracking social media accounts, internet browser searches, cellphones, and the latest facial recognition technology. They are careful to allow a sensible amount of freewill to remain for people to fall victim to various set trap doors (drugs, crime, and illicit activities).

Man is free, but his freedom ceases when he has no faith in it; and the greater power he ascribes to faith, the more he deprives himself of that power which god has given to him when he is at liberty to do everything he pleases, for he becomes a slave the moment he allows his actions to be ruled by passions. For the poor and middle-class its a forever battle to become wealthy enough for financial freedom; for the wealthy the battle is to keep that from happening because its their dependence that keeps them afloat.

Fear of destitution is the chief motive which inspires the daily work of most wage earners. The hope of possessing more wealth and power than any man ought to have, which is the corresponding motive of the rich, is quite as bad inits effects; it compels men to close their minds against justice and be complacent in the demise of the multitude for the gain of a few. It is only destine that the imbalance rectify itself.

32

World War $—Poor vs Rich

This chapter reference should be more appropriately titled Us vs. Them because of the impending war coming that won't draw color lines but survival lines. It is when the bottom of the system falls out or the increasing false security bubble bursts, that the poor and middle-classes will demand the common necessities of life from the few rich who has always profited from the majority. The bitterness and resentment will overflow from recognizing the many ways they have become more rich without contributing anything to the wealth of the communities they've held in dependence on their crumbs.

Economic slavery has bind down nine tenths of our population. The unjust distribution of wealth must be obviously an evil to those who are not prosperous. The love of riches, the desire of gain ever present for those without, and the pride of ambition takes possession of his mind to the exclusion of all else.

Whenever America attempts to have a conversation about race or poverty, it either starts out with victim-blaming or ends up with it. This borders on absurd. As if anyone truly believe that people want to be poor, that it's some kind of life ambition. Most black people want a life where they have the basic necessities—a decent job, good housing, and food on the table. We also want to be safe and have the best for our children, opportunities that lead to a bright future, and the pursuit of happiness without oppression.

Some writer has said that there are two classes of people, those who are driven to death, and those who are bored to death. There can be no sympathy between the rich and poor. There is an impassible gulf that can never be crossed. The man who has never known the want of money cannot know the sorrows and struggles of the poor. Each must go his own way, the poor man to his pallet of straw; the rich man to his bed of down.

Jesus says the meek shall inherit the land, but through my lifetime it seems to me the meek fertilizes the land I would argue. Freedom and wealth are difficult and responsible conditions to which men must be accustomed and socially trained from birth. But there is a contrary difference from those born into generational wealth off the blood, sweat, and tears of the less fortunate to those who rose from the squalid circumstances of poverty to wealth status. He is utterly self-made, and stands as a beacon of hope for those still in the social status he phoenix'd from. His heart still carries the empathy of his brethren dire struggles and powerless contempt.

In spite of apparent carelessness, indifference, and selfishness, the rich are not unmindful of the poor; they do not hate the poor, but they also would not trade places with them. The poor have no ill-feeling toward the rich in most instances; it is the circumstances in which engulfs their existence they hate. But it is the tyranny of the holders of power that contains the source of needless suffering and misfortune to very large sections of mankind; a power that remains in few hands, and tends, if anything, to grow more concentrated.

The wealthy uses x10 more resources than that of the poor. Asia and African nations have more of a greater population, but the few wealthy within all countries use more of the natural world resources than the collective poor throughout the world. From the highest to the lowest, almost all men are absorbed in the economic struggle; the struggle to acquire what is their due or to retain what is not their due. Material possessions, in fact or in desire, dominate our outlook.

In understanding the concept of it is better to be a lean freeman than a fat slave, we see the displacement of black people lies in the privilege of whites to move wherever and whenever they choose in total disregard for the impact on the environment (creating urban sprawl) or destroying black neighborhoods (gentrification), has kept this ability from us dually. This settler mentality has created a historical pattern of black removal that is duplicated in other cities.

As hard as black families have fought for decent housing and neighborhood stability, we're up against institutions and other forces which conspire to make our lives a living hell. The starting place is making sure there's never any permanency in where black people live.

Sinister designs to kil the Blackman's spirit, destroy his livelihood and criminalize him at the earliest convenience are a constant compounding factor in his existence.

The war has come as a challenge to all who desire abetter world. Men must learn to be conscious of the common interests of mankind in which all are at one, rather than of those supposed interests in which nations are divided. The priorities of this country are out of whack with a human agenda. The greatest wealth disparity continues to rob American families of their futures. Where 1 percent has the wealth and 99 percent creates the wealth. This is unacceptable. But so long as hatred, suspicion, and fear dominate the feelings of men toward each other. The only journey which the rich and the poor will take together, will be down and through the valley of the shadow of death.

33

From Bondage To Billions—
Combining Black Wealth

Whoever said money can't buy happiness must have not made enough money. Money is the tool by which man makes himself into the image he wants to be, it's by his aggressive nature that he achieves his ambitious goal, or demise.

There is nothing in the world so aggressive as the self-made man. The air with which he moves along, as though upon him depended the revolution of the world on its axis, and the safety and welfare of its inhabitants. He never allows himself, nor others, to forget the fact that he is self-made. It's the endless well from which he draws his motivation to continue his pursuits.

Every man, woman, and child is endowed with this aggressive nature, unfortunately whites used this nature to dominate and enslave African and Native-American slaves. This bondage has resulted in centuries of oppression by robbery, thievery, deception, and murder to acquire large tracts of land that now sits major cities and industries which employs to poor and middle-class citizens: the very descendants who would have inherited the land and by right to profit from it.

Today's modern slavery, be it by incarceration, or economically to slave away for low wages working for large corporations, proprietors, and the government. As a means to this end, the poor and middle-class needs to combine its resources and efforts in building our own economic facilities for our own people to take advantage of on reclaimed tracts of lands. Suing for the rights of entitlement for stolen land may be the first step. Similar actions to lawsuits brought by slaves who sued for their freedom in the antebellum period, in which families having to employ lawyers to negotiate the purchase of freedom for their loved one.It is for the release and relinquishment to free ourselves from oppression.

Owning and developing on our own lands agricultural, sewage, power, water, health, and economic systems. Our own built hospitals and healthcare systems that cater to cures and disease prevention instead of treatment and repair. Our own banks and financial investment institutions that focus solely or black businesses growth and prosperity in expansion, and fulfilling the needs of the community members without predatory lending motives. Our own cities, businesses, homes, stores, and education development schools and universities with proper education life lesson plans and educators to teach our true roots and the skills needed for black wealth and family security.

Needed is our own land tracts with highways, roads, and rail transportation network systems, airports and seaports, doing international commerce trade with other colored countries and nations. Moreover, our own United Nations recognized sovereignty interior government and legislation, along with our own military protection instillation, civil police force, and court justice system to oversee criminal accounts and civilian crimes and disputes; industries, plants, and factories that's beneficial to the surrounding residents.

Separation is required for the black race to thrive, not continued integration. Integration has been the cause of decline of black wealth starting many like instances in the 1960's. While there were early financial or political success stories, black people continued to meet racial hostility.

From the beginning, blacks refused to accept their state or status without resistance. For example, black people fought for the right to vote. An 1868 ballot proposition failed 2 to 1 but it was a clear indication that blacks were not going to accept second-class citizenship in spite of the daunting legal obstacles thrown in our paths.

Additionally, we must be mindful of the envious effects our growth has spurred in the past, taking sorrowful remembrance of the 1921 Greenwood-Tulsa, Oklahoma Massacre of blacks; better known as Black Wall Street that made up the more than 10,000 blacks, 600 businesses, 15 black millionaires that thrived amongst one another after the law enacted a covenant to restrict blacks to stay in a area just outside of Tulsa all of their own. The result enabled them to spend their money amongst each other.

Whites jealousy of their growth and development grew to heinous degree of white rioters who began to shoot black residents on sight, set fire to their homes and burn people alive. The precept being that a local Blackman being guilty of whistling at a white woman.

These white terrorists dragged blacks by cars, stole cars and owned planes to fly overhead to drop fire bombs on homes and businesses. In this they burned 35 blocks of homes and businesses to the ground. The national guard was brought in to help whites by arresting 6,000 black victims and affluent women and children fleeing into the woods, homeless and others captured held in detention centers through to winter. The state even denied blacks the ability to hold funeral processions to occur for the black victims, and instead made to bury victims in mass graves in order to cover up Tulsa's vile actions.

Historically it has shown it isn't black misbehavior that's a problem but Black success. Today, every dollar and cent combined with the knowledge and resolve to unite as a whole will be the only way to ensure our freedom from the current oppressive bondage we're held captive in. If it isn't Black owned tell them to get the fuck on. If we stop spending our money with them then things will have to change. Once you say fuck Cadillac, Walmart, Gucci, and Henessey, see what happens. Boycott them.

United we are strong but divided we're weak. Each individual must do their part to bring their mental capable state up to the standard of which is needed to achieve on to the next step of development of society. And it requires the resetting of ingrain perceptions, docility, fears, traumas, and self-absorption.

34

Regrets. Reflect. Reapply—StartingOver

The element of freedom dictates the ability to have free thought. This leads to cultivating those thoughts into actions that become impossible to ignore. Having foresight is an acquired skill. The ability to manifest your dreams and vision for a better future into plans and actions; and it must be worked on consistently like working out a muscle. The muscle tear repairs itself to become stronger.

Experiences in life are of a similar process. It was not intended that life should be all sunshine and no shadow. Dark cloud must appear in the life of each, and one of the great lessons of life is to learn to bear disappointments philosophically, not sit down with folded hands, and watch the clouds approaching until our vision becomes obscured. There is sunshine in the lives of each and everyone if they will but see it, and banish vain regrets and useless repinings.

Reflecting with immense regret blocks the vision to see the lessons needed to learn. Sometimes you don't know what you want to do until you know what you don't want to do. Still you must do. Applying your thoughts, hopes, wishes, desires—into everyday planned applications is required in getting to know yourself better than anyone else does know you.

In the world of dreams all are equal. It is an unreal world, true, but to many it is the happiest. Then comes the waking, and with the waking the regret of what "Might have been". To awake with regret to the cares which riches bring is living torment. We are all haunted by dreams and nightmares. The dreams of happiness and the nightmares of disappointments. Looking back upon our past and taking a retrospective glance at years gone by we find our lives have been made up not of great events, but of a succession of disappointments. Each one is haunted by a ghost or ideal which they are vainly striving to reach but seldom attain.

The garden of hope seems to bear well; we put forth our hands to reach the fruit and we find we have only the ashes of dead hopes. Instead, imagine first that the present is past, and, second, that the past may yet be changed and amended. Reflect on the experience and what it has taught you, and how to use it as an advantage in the future to clear emotional baggage inhabiting mental space, enabling self from living life the way its suppose to.

Reflecting on these regrets, mishaps and mistakes, and viewing it from an objective point of narrative view, imagine the result you rather it had been, then think that result through to the next regret, and so onward to the present. Then live your life in that imagined result; working towards it in its totality.

As an exercise; at a quiet solitude time of day, think back to the very first regret you ever had, even if from childhood, write out what happen, what you did or didn't do that you wish you've done differently, and imagine the result that would have occurred in the favor that you wish. Then proceed forward towards the next up until the current moment. Review your new life results, then work towards making those results a reality.

If you have not done anything worthy of being recorded, at least write something worthy of being read. Worthy or not, your life is your subject, and your subject is your life. In the meaning of this process, appreciate the new found peace and calm, and what has been learnt about the world and acquired philosophy of life. Freedom is much more appreciated when you have been imprisoned, both physically and mentally.

In all grace, I can state going to prison saved my life. Breaking the bondages of self-sabotage required self-reflection. Solitude allowed this to happen. Clearing out the haze in which most have traveled endlessly through pitfall after pitfall, you will arrive at the profound choice to accept your past mistakes and implement the changes needed; or you can continue on the path of self-destruction.

35

Sweet Nightmares—Wake Up Or Sleep Forever

Occasionally the public awakes to a realization of their power over both courts and lawyers, that they are their elected employees, and are suppose to respond to their needs and demands. When the response is favorable for the people (usually only short-term), then happens a revolution in procedure and something is accomplished. When the response is unfavorable for the people, it s usually too late to correct the injury, and the grossly delayed fix is like trying to cure the cancer of a patient while they lay on their death bed in the last stages of life.

To win our freedom we must be strong. Let us keep this in our mind, that our strength lies in numbers, concentration, unity, reliance on one another and our chiefs, leaders, and disciplined well organized army front of like minded individuals; purging our lives of the untruthful history accounts meant to discourage any inspiration to rise greater than our oppressive standards. Recognize immediately men having two tongues, saying one thing and meaning another in efforts to lead you blindly to your demise.

Having common sense is the most valuable gift with which man can be endowed. It is the very essence of genius, for it consists in the application of intelligence to every detail, and the highest order of intellect can accomplish no more than that. As with the growing collective consciousness that police and state-sanctioned terrorism is unbated in our communities, and that all African Americans have been criminalized regardless of our economic and social station in life. Even as it may to be enlighten to the current circumstances is one thing, but actually working towards making things change is another.

We cannot change the history behind us and we definitely shouldn't try to re-write or gloss over the gross injustices, but we have the power to determine what kind of future we want in the region and ultimately, in this country. It is never too late to right the wrongs of this society no matter whoever was on the receiving side of the wrongs. To those living in a dream world, it can be provided by the nightmares of others.

The minds of many adults are still in their infancy, only seeing in a small circle of the things surrounding their immediate close proximity, not understanding the bigger picture of things around them.

Taking an observation of the years 2014, 2015, and 2016 seen a spike in racially motivated violent incidents between cops and black's that went public:

• 2014, Aug.9, a white police officer fatally shot an unarmed black 18 year old Michael   Brown in Ferguson, MO, precipitating violent protests; the grand jury declined to indict the officer.

• Tamir Rice, a black 12 year old holding a pellet gun, was fatally shot and killed by a white police officer, Nov. 22, 2014, in Cleveland, OH; the grand jury declined to indict.

• On Dec.3, a grand jury decided not to indict a New York City police officer for using a non-regulation chokehold to detain Eric Garner, a Blackman who died July 17th in custody. These same officers went on to complain they were unable to secure employment within Police Departments because of the incidents. But what about the people whom they killed innocently? They would never again have the chance to work any kind of employment anywhere. What about the families they left behind who had to take on additional jobs to provide for children whom parent life was loss at your hands?

• On Dec.20, a Blackman shot and killed two New York City police officers in their patrol car then killed himself.

• March 4, 2015, the Justice Department released a report exposing widespread mistreatment of African Americans by Ferguson, MO. police and court system, mandating policy changes.

• The2015 Apr.19th death of a Blackman, Freddie Gray, from an injury sustained in a Baltimore police van spurred riots and led to the indictment of six officers but no convictions resulted.

• 2016 protests followed the fatal shooting of a Blackman in each of two unrelated encounters with police in Baton Rouge,LA. July 5th, and a St. Paul,MN. suburb, July 6th, but no charges brought in Baton Rouge incident; and a 2017 trial n MN ended in officer's acquittal. In attacks by two unconnected gunman, apparently motivated by revenge, five police officers were killed by a sniper, July 7th, in Dallas,TX , and three officers were killed in an ambush, July 17th, in Baton Rouge.

- A Justice Department report released Aug.10th, 2016 that concluded that Baltimore Police routinely used excessive force against black residents.
- Riots broke out in Milwaukee,WI. Aug.13th–15th, 2016 following a police shooting of an armed Blackman fleeing a traffic stop. The officer, who was black, was tried and acquitted.
- An unarmed black motorists was fatally shot Sept.16th, 2016 in an encounter with police in Tulsa,OK. The officer was acquitted of manslaughter.
- In Charlotte,NC. Sept. 20th, 2016, a police officer fatally shot an allegedly armed Blackman. No charges brought against the officer.
- A U.S. Justice Dept. investigation of the Chicago Police Dept., launched after a video of a white officer fatally shooting a black teen 16 times, Laquan McDonald, sparked protests, and found in Jan.2017 that officers used excessive force too often and without repercussions. The officer Jason Van Dyke was indicted, convicted, and sentenced to 6 years in prison.

It must be acknowledged by using the given faculties of thinking and observation to the best advantage to arrive at the formed conclusions about the operations outset against you. Where your house is located determines what schools you have access to, how healthy you will be and your employment opportunities. Most people outside of these communities never see or hear of the racial strife between its citizens and the police until incidents happen like those involving Mike Brown, Trevon Martin, Laquan McDonald, and so many other murdered by white cops. Only then do outsiders get a glimpse of what life is like for black citizens.

Years of political disenfranchisement, broken promises, police harassment and economic injustices eventually takes its toll. It's a utter shame you gotta wait until its dark out to see who really with you, but we must forget what lies behind and keep pressing forward in learning, in growing, in changing, in offensive position for at the very least, a last stand, and making sacrifices that are more inspiring than a great victory. Instinct and intuition becomes the safest guide, and following it leads to remarkable accuracy more than stumbling around in the darkness of confusion and ignorance.

Over the previous thirty-four chapters my intentions have been to allow the reader's great principles to shine through, and inform the rest, that illumines the mind of the individual, that clarifies and invigorates—puts the mind in focus, gets the facts of existence into perspective, and gives the individual everything in its right place and true proportion. It brings a man to the point where he does not dispute but believes.

Personally, for years I was drinking in deep despair, I could not understand the want in my soul, nor the origin of my oppression, while I had been looking for panacea for its cure, I wasn't until the great light streams of inner enlightenment, that I realized instead I should have been open to receiving something I could only find in myself. Nature had given me a very lively mind, and a very susceptible heart, and neither of them could be kept quiet against the visions I foreseen coupled with the desire to learn more about the inception of the oppressions of my race. This excited uneasiness in my mind, and kindled resentment with the more I discovered.

While I slept, whispers and displays of visual wisdom held siege to my mind and heart. Awakening I recounted all of the wonderful journeys I had taken to a parallel world, but one without the oppressions of my people. These constant visions made me question can there be another god besides god? Who is there to pray to when your prayers go on unanswered? Who listens to the soul distressed when it calls on him, and who relieves its suffering and makes you whole again, if there is the possibility? The only answer I received was self.

It is self that must bring himself to the higher plane of god like abilities; healing the sick; feeding the hungry; housing the homeless; giving light to the lost, and unite enemies into friends. It has been a powerful relentless everlasting vision. A power of vision is in us all, where true philosophy is wonderful and inspiring. He acquires that vision is impervious to argument; it is not that he despises argument, on the contrary, he always uses it to its full strength. Who has been a doubter, a faulter, a failure, will become a believer, a fighter, a conqueror.

In my significance to make accounts of the presented civilization ill's, opposition will attempt to label me as a theorists or radicalist for my apparent views. But they miss the point purposely by neglecting to address the very issues I speak on, and instead concentrate on the orator, not the message being spoke. In greater explanation; the theorists propounds a view to which he must convert the world; the philosopher has a rule of life to immediately put into practice. It is like a new and wonderful vitality in the blood to have over and above a new penetrating argument in the mind.

The unbeliever, near by, still muddled by his cold theories, will argue and debate till his intellect is in a tangle, he fails to see that a man of intellectual agility might frame a theory and argue it out ably, and then suddenly turn over and with equal dexterity argue the other side.

In this book I could've pointed out the multitude flaws and faults that are contrary objectives to the points I have made. The White Plague could have very well been and inevitable destination against a race of socially and technologically ignorant people who means for a life of servitude because of there docility. The Seeds of Oppression were not planted in malice but in superior forethought for the future. Maybe there wasn't an Miseducation Protocol but slaves and the descendants from with are just inherit-ably incapable of superior mental development. False Idols could be needed as keeping people motivated and the Martyred Heroes of the past are just a unique few unicorns.

The divisions between men are a natural make up of human civilization and cultures are created and lost over time as a means of superior development. One could believe the drug problem and opioid crises are a needed evil in America to combat the problem of mental disorders and boredom.

To the person docile and naïve enough to give away his rightful land and slavishly toil away for free, shouldn't they be taken advantage of then? And Snitches help solve cases and put dangerous criminals behind bars. Aggressive police and prosecutors are modern day heroes helping to end violent crimes against the public. The Slave Ship styled jail processes should be made uncomfortable and hard in effect to deter recidivism. As well as the Majority Public Defenders accurately give adequate defenses for defendants, and the ones who fall through the cracks may have just been lost causes to begin with.

As I said before; ignorance of the law is not an excuse, so to be knowledgable about laws that affect you is your own responsibility. The public at large are fed up with criminals who constantly commit crimes, and it's necessary to respond to it appropriately by keeping them incarcerated. Far off Prisons, being left from the loved ones and support of loved ones, the costs while incarcerated—are all the consequences of committing crimes.

Tax Dollars spent on incarcerated persons also provides other important state funded programs to assist persons returning from prison and drug rehabilitation facilities. And Poor and middle-class generations, old and young, are the personal handicaps of the minority's concern.

In recognizing the totality of human evolution, it would be a natural occurrence to be propounded by so many technological advances that the average American would be so distracted, he could be considered a product of automation, akin to a machine.

One could also argue to be poor is a mindset and their are plenty of opportunities to rise to better circumstances if they but take advantage of them like the rich has. Incidentally, if you don't take up action for yourself, then they figure you stupid then.

Being black in America shouldn't be an automatic death sentence. The question should be why are you so afraid of my growth and potential to excel? The recent death of George Floyd at the hands of a white officer when he applied his knee to his neck for more than eight minutes isn't a new kind of murder carried out by white officers. They've had their foot, knees, batons, and guns on our necks for centuries. A possible proper punishment for officers who carry out deeds such as this should be hanged publicly. Jason Van Dyke should have died by a firing squad. Texas Police officer, Amber Guyger, should be open fired upon surprisingly as she eats her last meal. That's equal measure of justice.

All in all, it is my message to my brethren to take at heart the living nightmares he is subjected to daily and wake up. Wake up Blackman! Wake up to save your brothers and sisters lost and in desperate need of your aid and assistance. Wake up Blackman from your slumber of wickedness, weakness, and shame. Wake up and rise to your birthright greatness as kings and queens, and reclaim your inherited kingdoms. Wake up and rise above the restrictions, confinements, oppressions, distractions held siege against you meant to prevent your god given abilities to lead, to teach, to protect your families, villages, and communities, you've been asleep far too long.

I know you're scared, shell shocked, ashamed, angry, heart-broken, scarred, taken to depths so low that you do not know which way is up, but I ensure you it is not up that you should look but inside yourselves you should seek and take claim to great power instilled into each and every one of you for which your enemy does not want you to realize, for he is fearful to a great extent of the day you discover your powers and rise above his propaganda's, his drugs, his diseases, his prisons, his welfares, his religions, his vile women, and his oppressions to keep you deaf, blind, dumb, and distracted to whats rightfully yours to begin with.

It is your time to wake up Blackman, it is time to reign supreme.

36

Breaking Branches—What Needs To Happen

If patient waiting, prayers, and longing have power to affect disembodied spirits, my faith will surely be rewarded. But much work is required. Painful feelings of anger, sadness, rage, and hopelessness have not lost their potency within the black community. New generation activists, radicals and organizers will have to become a symbol of resistance to police violence and white supremacy everywhere. Challenging racism in the streets, in police departments and in the courts.

The social justice movement is as much about changing hearts and minds as it is changing laws and policies. Who believe in freedom cannot rest. Men must come together who believes in complete freedom, nor deadlocked with others who are so satisfied with partial freedom. Immediate action must be consistently taken to attain the ultimate goal: Freedom from oppression.

Take the sails of oppression and subject it to targeted attacks; and by inviting it into your life and you'll succeed in completely conquering it. Fighting for justice and humanity and the weak and the poor and the oppressed until change is met as its normalcy. They demand our sympathy and our support from every willing and able person. The best way to cure the disheartened and obstinate laborer is to give him just wages and kind treatment.

The fact is, reasonable and kind treatment will generally produce a great and beneficial change in vicious animals as well as vicious men. So shouldn't prisoners and released convicts be considered with the same grace?

Our perception and empathy of others is needed to evolve to a great degree. In its change our judgement should be relaxed. People of a different circumstance says to itself after hearing the sin of some poor man; "I am holier than that person, I have never sinned in that way", forgetful of the fact that they have never been tempted or victimized in the same way, nor have had to contend with the same struggles for whom they judge.

Here is a poor man who has been sorely tired and tempted, instead show him his error and help him to do right. Never forgetting a kindness received from another, but forget at once a kindness done to another. Love gives and receives, and keeps no account on either side. Blessed are they who expect little.

Differing ideals should be combined as similar tribes to unite into a strong confederacy. Separately we are weak, and a foe could do us much harm; united we would be so strong that no one could trouble us. Each could still remain independent in managing its own affairs, but together should be one great power which would help all.

Additionally, these inner city communities empty households needs their leaders back. These black men have to be out there to take control of their family, and must accept the responsibility for its direction. There are already too many single mothers and irresponsible dads in our culture.

The Blackman has gotten so down trodden upon and beaten into a lazy effort that he has left the direction of the family in the woman's hand. Life has shown us that this is not a good decision. They must work on getting back to their family so that another black family is not left without a leader.

Our young boys and girls today are lost. You have to go and be the man so that your woman and your child will respect you. In turn they will understand their role in society.

Laws need to be lobbied to pass for reversing the ill-effects of mass incarceration. Too many jails are filled with black men whose families are put into a circle that creates weak men and disrespectful women. A young woman will always have difficulties respecting a man if she has never seen that man in a responsible role. A man must always protect his family, it is up to you to accept the responsibility for your family and guide its members in the right direction.

The love and support of their women are needed to encourage the men to be men as well, not memories. Until we do that as a people our young children will always be dying in the streets.

To be relevant to the social justice movement, you must be relevant to young people, which is our future. Factors such as poverty, unemployment, economic inequality and failed educational systems are contributors to crime. These elements make for a future unfulfilled. A failure on all of us then.

In closing, we must always contradict an authoritative statement and research given facts that seem inconclusive to your intuition. Remember that the progress of the world depends on your knowing better than your elders.

End